TABLE OF CONTENTS

INTRODUCTION 1

CHAPTER 1: THE REALITY OF BESTSELLING BOOKS 5

CHAPTER 2: LAYING THE GROUNDWORK 14

CHAPTER 3: BUILD AN ARC TEAM 43

CHAPTER 4: SET UP PRE-ORDERS 69

CHAPTER 5: RUNNING AMAZON ADS 77

CHAPTER 6: PUBLISHING THE AUDIOBOOK 90

CHAPTER 7: MARKETING & PROMOTION 95

CHAPTER 8: BOOK LAUNCH DAY 111

CHAPTER 9: POST-BOOK LAUNCH ITEMS 119

CONCLUSION 121

THE BESTSELLER BOOK LAUNCH CHECKLIST 124

A SMALL ASK	127
ABOUT THE AUTHOR	128
SPECIAL THANKS	130
RESOURCES	132
REFERENCES	136

BESTSELLER BOOK LAUNCH PLAN

THE ULTIMATE GUIDE TO BECOMING A BESTSELLING AUTHOR ON THE WORLD'S LARGEST ONLINE RETAILER

DALE L. ROBERTS

Bestseller Book Launch Plan: The Ultimate Guide to Becoming a Bestselling Author on the World's Largest Online Retailer

All rights reserved.

Copyright ©2025 One Jacked Monkey, LLC

- Ebook ISBN: 978-1-63925-063-9
- Paperback ISBN: 978-1-63925-064-6
- Hardcover ISBN: 978-1-63925-065-3
- Audiobook ISBN: 978-1-63925-066-0

No part of this book may be reproduced in any form by any electronic or mechanical means, including information storage and retrieval systems, without permission in writing from the copyright owner, except by a reviewer who may quote brief passages in a review.

Disclaimer

The information provided in this book is accurate to the best of the author's knowledge at the time of publication. However, due to the evolving nature of the topics discussed, some information may change over time. The author makes no representations or warranties regarding the accuracy or completeness of the information contained within this book. It is the reader's responsibility to verify any facts or details, and to conduct further research or consult updated sources as needed.

Some recommended links in this book are part of affiliate programs. If you purchase a product through one of the links, then I get a portion of each sale. It doesn't affect your cost and greatly helps support the cause. If you have any reservations about buying a product through my affiliate link, then Google a direct link and bypass the affiliate link.

STAY AHEAD IN SELF-PUBLISHING!

Imagine having a step-by-step guide to launching a successful book. Now imagine getting even more—news, insider tips, and special deals—all delivered straight to your inbox.

Join thousands of other authors and get exclusive access to my email newsletter. As a bonus, you'll also receive the **Bestseller Book Launch Checklist**, your free cheat sheet to simplify your book launch and keep you on track.

Subscribe now at DaleLinks.com/Checklist.

Win **awards** and get **reviews** for **your book**

25% off your first purchase

bookawardpro.com

"I've used dozens of book cover design services over the last ten years, and none compare to the level of quality and professionalism that Miblart delivers."

— **Dale L. Roberts** —

Miblart - a book cover design company for self-published authors

Designers who specialize in different genres	Unlimited number of revisions
No deposit to get started	You can pay in installments

GET A BOOK COVER THAT WILL BECOME YOUR N°1 MARKETING TOOL

Excellent

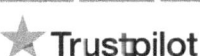 4.9

 Trustpilot

UnBlock Writers Block
Trouble Finishing Your Book? Or Even Starting?

Meet **Dibbly Create.** Your All-in-1 A.I. companion for publishing your book

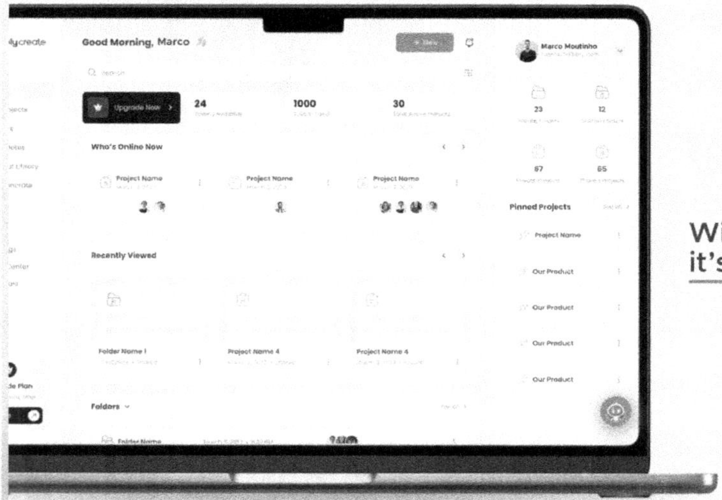

With Dibbly, it's done.

- ✓ Research
- ✓ Writing
- ✓ Editing
- ✓ Formatting
- ✓ Proofreading
- ✓ Designing
- ✓ Publish-Ready

Yes,
I Need Help Finishing my Book

Try for Free!
Scan the QR Code or visit dibbly.com/create

Next level tools to help you grow.

Whether you're an aspiring author or international bestseller, we've got the tools to help you publish faster, distribute wider and manage your business easier.

Learn more by going to **d2d.tips/dale** and read on to discover some of what sets D2D apart:

- ✓ **Automated end-matter**
- ✓ **New Release Notifications for readers**
- ✓ **Payment Splitting for contributors**
- ✓ **Scheduled price changes**
- ✓ **Smashwords store coupons**
- ✓ **Universal Book Links via Books2Read.com**

 **It's print-on-demand reimagined.**

Create a paperback on draft2digital.com from your existing ebook with just a few clicks, and **create a full, wrap-around book cover from your ebook cover**. It really is that easy!

 **THE indie bookstore.**

Massive annual sales, self-serve promotion tools, and the **industry's best royalty rates** of up to 80% list. Readers love discovering breakout indie authors at smashwords.com.

INTRODUCTION

Writing and publishing a bestselling book is a huge accomplishment for any author. Just knowing you've sold enough copies to earn the title—one that stays with you forever—is reason enough to celebrate. Some might compare it to hitting a game-winning home run in the Baseball World Series.

Instead of training for years or playing an entire season, all I had to do was sell a certain number of books in a specific time.

I became a bestselling author on Amazon in January 2016, shortly after the launch of my fitness book compilation, *An Ultimate Home Workout Plan Bundle*. A close friend, Kevin Allen, challenged me to hit the #1 spot in my book's categories on Amazon. I loved the idea of hitting #1, but I had no resources, no real following, and next to no money.

For two years prior, my wife and I had struggled to make ends meet. Thankfully, she had a semi-successful Amazon FBA business that kept our heads above water. The meager earnings I got from my books weren't enough to pay all the bills. We treaded water for a long time, so much that I had to reconsider returning to the day job I'd left in order to pursue a writing career.

By the time early 2016 rolled around, I was frustrated, disappointed, and terrified that my lifelong dream would not pan out after all. That book was going to be my last effort, that final hurrah before giving up on my pipe dream.

The marketing strategy for my fitness book was simple—promote my book in every imaginable place online, from Facebook to Twitter to website promos. My logic was if I could direct traffic and gather some sales, Amazon would shine a spotlight on my book and send additional buyers.

From December 10, 2015, to February 3, 2016, I sold 121 books, accumulated 61,504 Kindle page reads, and saw 163 downloads of the free book. Since I had priced my book absurdly low at $0.99 for most of that promotional run, I only earned about $0.35 per sale. Of course, I was getting jack squat from the free downloads. At the time, the cost per page read through the KDP Select Program was less than half a cent per page.

Though the results weren't massive, they were enough to place my book at #1 in Aerobics and Ab Workouts, and thirteenth in Weight Training on the Amazon Best Seller lists. While I may have won the battle, I was far from winning the war. Could I repeat this success? And could I maintain it with the same strategies?

SPOILER ALERT: I repeated this success with subsequent publications through trial and error, learning and implementing more proven tactics and strategies for successful book launches. In fact, I achieved much better results with later launches.

Based on the numbers, hitting #1 in a specific category on Amazon was surprisingly achievable, far easier than I originally expected. I'd always been told that it takes thousands of sales to make a bestseller list, like those of USA Today or the New York Times, but this was a clear reminder that success on Amazon is within reach.

Yes, if an author wants their book to rank in the top 100 ebooks on Amazon (US), it typically requires selling thousands of copies in a day. To hit the #1 spot, you'll need to sell around 6,390 copies within 24 hours. However, this number can fluctuate based on factors like competing releases and the sales of established ebooks. The estimate of 6,390 copies comes from the Kindlepreneur's Amazon Book Sales Calculator, which tracks real-time sales trends.

A common concern is whether the strategies I used in 2016 are still effective today. While some of my methods are now outdated, the fundamentals still apply. You won't have to spam social media, pester friends and family, or pay for obsolete or ineffective promotional services.

After interviewing over 125 successful authors and experts from both traditional and self-publishing, I've gathered the best strategies to help you sell more books—without using ineffective methods or bothering your friends. No, I won't have you leaning on your friends and family, because as you'll learn later, they'll actually work against your mission to get and maintain your title in the bestseller lists.

Authors who craft and execute a solid book launch strategy, just as carefully as they write and refine their manuscript, set themselves up for success. However, there's a big myth in the industry: the idea that "if you build it, they will come." That's far from the truth. Writing a book, whether in a competitive or niche market, doesn't automatically mean readers will come looking for it.

Writing the first draft takes time, but the real work starts once you have a finished manuscript. Editing, proofreading, formatting, and all the other tasks follow, and they are essential steps in preparing your book for publication. Marketing and promotion shouldn't wait until after you hit publish—it's a continuous effort before, during, and after the launch. Unfortunately, that's where many authors give up, opting to publish and hope for the best instead.

Not you though, right? I suspect you picked up this book for a good reason. You want to know—scratch that, you *need* to know—how to launch a book into the top of the Amazon Best Sellers Lists so you can proudly boast your newfound status as a bestselling author.

You'll find all the links to the sites, tools, services, and resources mentioned throughout this book in the Resources section at the back. I've compiled everything in one place for easy access, so you can focus on implementing the strategies shared here. Be sure to check it out when you reach the end of the book.

Before you can claim the title of bestselling author and proudly defend your status, let's explore what it means to be a bestseller, both on and off Amazon. We'll then dive into the fundamentals of a bestseller book launch. To wrap it all up, you'll receive my bestseller book launch checklist to ensure you have a foolproof action plan when it's time to publish your next book.

Flip that page so we can dig right in!

CHAPTER 1:
THE REALITY OF BESTSELLING BOOKS

In 2016, Brent Underwood exposed what some would call the farce of a bestselling book on Amazon. He showed how he could publish any book and list it in some obscure category to claim ownership of the number one bestselling book. His tongue-in-cheek nod to the absurdity came through *Putting My Foot Down*, a "book" that was literally a picture of his foot. That's it. He ordered a couple of copies of his ebook, then landed at the top of the Amazon Best Seller list for Transpersonal Psychology.[i]

Despite my lack of understanding of "transpersonal psychology," I feel confident that a picture of a foot hardly belongs on a virtual bookshelf reserved for more deserving titles. Not long after launching his book, Brent updated the interior with more context and re-categorized his book into Parody, where it sat at a rank more appropriate for a book that sells a couple of copies on rare occasions.

I applaud Brent for exposing Amazon's dirty little secret, but we can only partially blame the online retailer. The real responsibility lies with authors to understand and disclose the true value of the bestseller tag. While gaming the system in an obscure category may work, achieving success in a more competitive category should be considered a true victory. Ultimately, it's up to you how you approach this.

Hitting the top 10,000 books on Amazon can be seen as an accomplishment, but not everyone will view it the same way. For some, a category bestseller ribbon on Amazon might seem like a fleeting badge, reflecting a book's performance in a specific category at a single point in time. This achievement can still be valuable for marketing and boosting visibility, but landing a book in Amazon's top-performing titles with sustained sales and broader visibility carries more weight. The significance of these ranks may not be fully understood by the general public, and the true value of the title "bestselling author" can vary depending on the category achieved. For authors, landing in a competitive category with strong sales may be more prestigious than being a bestseller in a niche with limited competition.

In recent years, Amazon KDP has become much more vigilant about removing or blocking books that are incorrectly categorized. Account holders can choose up to three categories per publication based on the type of book (e.g., ebooks, print books), but they must adhere to the platform's Terms & Conditions. You'll discover through a quick browse through the terms that:

> *You must ensure that all metadata you provide to us is current, complete, and accurate.*[ii]

Amazon isn't too keen about category abuse. Amazon puts these categories in place so that the products are more discoverable and accessible to customers. You can imagine how annoying—or even possibly unsettling—it is to see a car repair manual in a children's book category. People often refer to this practice as category squatting, where some authors game the system through placement to earn a hollow accolade. Amazon will actively block books and, sometimes, terminate accounts because of improper category selection.

The challenge is selecting the proper categories and creating a strategy that will position your book at the top of the bestseller lists for those categories. That way, when you boast about your bestseller status, you have proof that it's not just a fluke or an easily manipulated category that only requires two sales to hit the #1 spot. Remember: the more strategic your category selection, the more likely your sales will reflect your book's true success, helping you maintain that top spot.

ARE BESTSELLER LISTS A FARCE?

What if I told you that some bestseller lists, like the New York Times Bestseller List, don't work the way most people think? While the list itself is a respected metric, what many don't realize is how the NYT compiles its data. It doesn't simply count pure sales; instead, it weighs certain types of sales more heavily, influencing which books make the list.

Bestseller lists should accurately reflect the books that sell the most within a specific time frame, typically a week. However, Amazon's bestseller lists are updated hourly,[iii] making them different from traditional lists like the New York Times, which usually require selling thousands of books through retailers that report sales to these lists. For example, NPD BookScan tracks all book sales in the US, primarily relying on sales reported by bookstores, though this process can be tricky.

Let's say you're aiming for a bestseller list, and you think that selling a large number of copies in a short time is all it takes. You might ask a friend to bulk order thousands of copies from a local bookstore, hoping those sales count toward the bestseller rankings. The truth is the system detects these tactics. Bulk orders can flag books, damaging their credibility and affecting how sales contribute to bestseller rankings.

Having bestseller status doesn't pay the bills—sales do. More sales allow you to reinvest into marketing, which helps increase your rank. But focusing on sales, not rank, is key to long-term success. Stop obsessively refreshing your browser or checking your rank in the newspaper. You can track your ranking effectively without wasting time on redundant tasks.

Historically, *The New York Times* (*NYT*) faced significant scrutiny for not solely reflecting in-store book sales on their bestseller list. In 1983, author William Blatty of *The Exorcist* sued the *NYT* after they excluded his book *Legion* from their list, despite it allegedly selling 84,000 copies. Blatty argued that this exclusion hurt the book's sales, prompting him to seek $9 million in damages. *NYT* defended its process, revealing that their bestseller list was editorially curated, not based solely on sales data.[iv] This means the New York Times cherry-picks which books make the list, making the bestseller rank more about their editorial judgment than raw sales numbers.

Some folks are quick to look down on Amazon Bestseller status, but they need to scrutinize the other bestseller lists equally. Is it easier to hit bestselling status on Amazon than it is on *USA Today* or *NYT*? Absolutely! You're going to need a solid launch strategy that leverages every avenue and resource you have. No, I'm not telling you to take out a mortgage on the house. Be practical and smart. You're going to need more than a publish-and-pray strategy. One in a million authors might launch with little fanfare and still get results, but most of us will need to be scrappy and resourceful.

WHY AMAZON'S BEST SELLER RANK IS BETTER THAN YOU KNOW

One of the other distinctions between the Amazon bestseller list and the other big name bestseller lists is near real-time data. Popular lists like the *New York Times* publish the list weekly, whereas the Amazon bestseller lists update hourly. On Amazon, product sales ebb and flow because traffic and sales are always coming and going. You will see some books at the top of the charts (i.e., perennial sellers), but even those don't stay at the top forever. Eventually, another book is going to come along and replace it.

The beauty of leveraging Amazon is the factor of sales relevance. If a book sells consistently well, Amazon will serve it to more potential customers. Should those recommendations convert into sales, Amazon recommends your book to even more customers. Better yet, if you bring your own "guests" to the "party," Amazon is more likely to invite more of their own "guests." Meaning, when you actively send potential readers to your product pages to buy your book, Amazon willingly puts in equal effort without prompting.

In order to get that type of reciprocal love, you'll need to better understand the system Amazon uses for its products. It's actually simple, though most new authors might find it overwhelming. That's where this book comes in!

The Amazon Best Seller Rank (ABSR) is a detailed list of products organized into a hierarchy. The first level is the category, which is a broad classification, like Romance, Self-Help, or History. Below that, you'll find subcategories that further define the specific type of content, such as Historical Romance or Personal Development. Some subcategories may break down even further into additional layers. The final level is placement, which is the most specific rank within that hierarchy, showing the book's position within its category and subcategory.

Fun Fact: When you see a category breakdown like the previous example, it's also referred to as a browse path.

On the Amazon Help page for KDP Categories,[v] they outline the anatomy of a category with this example:

- Category = History
- Subcategory = History > US History
- Placement = History > US History > 19th Century

Visit Amazon and select any book. As long as the book has had a sale, one to three categories will appear in the Product Details section for that title. Publishers can select these categories, and Amazon sometimes automatically assigns them based on the category and backend keyword choices.

Here's where it gets interesting: The bestseller tag isn't just about where your book lands in its final category. While it's easiest to land the bestseller tag at the placement level, it gets progressively harder as you move up the hierarchy. At the broadest level, like the Kindle Store (product level), you might need to sell 6,390 copies to reach #1. As you narrow the browse path down to a category, like Romance or Business & Money, it becomes a little easier to claim the top spot. The more specific the category gets—down to subcategories and, ultimately, placement—the easier it is to hit #1, because there's less competition.

The first category classification is the broadest, meaning it has the most competition for a book's sales rank. Reaching the top 20 in a category, such as Romance or Self-Help, indicates strong performance within that category. However, ranking in the top 20 of a product category like Kindle or Books represents overall sales rank and likely requires thousands of sales per day.

Amazon registers each book sale according to product type and subcategory. Every author aims for that coveted top spot in Amazon's overall rankings—the ultimate bragging rights for dominating the platform. The more sales you get, the closer you move to the #1 spot. Conversely, fewer sales mean you drift farther away. However, as the category breaks down into narrower subcategories and placement, the competition gets smaller and more specific. This can make it easier to reach #1, like in a niche category with little competition, requiring fewer sales to hit the top.

Is this victory as prestigious as dominating the overall ranking? That's up to you. But keep in mind, you're still technically a bestselling author. And, when you tell others you're an Amazon bestselling author, most people outside of the industry will likely be impressed—just as they would with any bestseller title.

Understanding the difference between book sales, checkouts, and downloads is crucial. While sales are typically the primary factor in determining a book's bestseller status, Amazon's KDP Select Program offers an exclusive digital lending service. When someone checks out an ebook for the first time through this program, Amazon registers that checkout as a sale, which can impact the ABSR. This means that, technically, you don't have to sell a single ebook to achieve bestseller status on Amazon. You can still earn royalties based on checkouts and page reads through the program.

Sadly, for the author that reward is often less than half a cent per page read and largely relies on a monthly pool of subscriber payments. While the KDP Select Global Fund has grown to over $60 million (August 2024[vi]), the amount paid per page read has gradually decreased. In fact, book marketing expert Joe Solari shared how most authors aren't looking at the bigger picture. The amount paid per page read has gradually decreased while the subscriber pool has increased.[vii] When accounting for inflation and the decreasing value of the dollar, authors are earning a fraction of what they used to.

Does the KDP Select Program offer an advantage for enrolled ebooks? Absolutely. Enrolling in KDP Select provides marketing opportunities and can influence your book's rank when customers check it out. However, it's important to make the most of these benefits. Relying solely on pages read to generate significant income might not be the most effective strategy, especially if you're not seeing the returns you expect. If you're aiming for serious success and feel dissatisfied with what KDP Select offers, you may want to reconsider its use.

Will enrolling your ebook in the KDP Select Program help with your bestseller book launch? Yes, but it's not mandatory. I recommend that new authors or hobbyists consider enrolling their ebook in the program for the first ninety days after publication. If they see any benefits, they can always renew. If it doesn't work out, they can simply remove the ebook from KDP Select and distribute it everywhere else.

My preference leans toward diversification. While KDP Select can provide an advantage in ranking your ebook higher on Amazon, I prioritize making my ebook available in as many places as possible. My main goal is to reach more readers and generate enough revenue to support my business. If you share similar goals, you'll find my approach to be practical and easy to execute with a little planning and trial and error at each stage of your launch.

CHAPTER 2:
LAYING THE GROUNDWORK

Before you ever consider hitting the publish button, you must have certain elements in place to ensure greater chances of success. All the marketing in the world won't help you sell more books without getting the basics of your book launch right. Start with a high-quality book that has undergone professional editing, beta reader reviews, proofreading, formatting, and features a professional cover design. In the event you can't afford to hire a pro, network and collaborate with other authors in the same position. You'll get an even greater advantage working with authors within your niche, so you get sound advice and helpful feedback.

Every author needs to scrutinize every aspect of their book launch before executing. This includes the book's pertinent details like the keywords, book description, and cover design. But it also comes back to the actual content you're producing.

You can be a terrible author with bestseller status, but the reality is few readers are going to give you a second chance. No matter what level of work you put into the whole launch, never lose sight of what is most important—the reader.

You shouldn't alienate or offend your target audience, so remember as long as you're doing right by your readership, then the steps you're taking to get there are good. My aim for this book is to provide you with proven, actionable advice, clear insights, and achievable goals to help you build a successful publishing strategy. This book is not just a guide to launching a bestseller on Amazon, it's a realistic view of what actually goes into becoming a bestselling author.

In short, your book can't just be good or average, it has to be great. The foundation that holds your entire business together is a great book—or backlog of books—that readers can enjoy and share with other readers, too. After you get the manuscript right, it's time to look at what keeps your book afloat through sales.

How do you get more book sales? Through discovery, aesthetics, and marketing copy. Without elements for discovery embedded in your metadata, no one will have the luxury of finding you—let alone knowing you exist. After all, Amazon is a *massive* platform that doesn't just specialize in book sales. Putting another product onto the Amazon Marketplace isn't reason enough for browsing customers to find you.

Enter keywords.

Keywords are a string of words or a phrase that summarizes what customers can expect in your product. Use the right keywords, and you'll open your book's listing to a specific audience. Select the wrong keywords and you'll be serving your book to the wrong crowd, therefore losing any real momentum on the Amazon Marketplace.

Even though discovery should be your top priority, the fact is you're going to need a compelling reason for browsing customers to select your book after they've found it over the millions of other products on Amazon. Your cover design is key to selling your book. Sure, some authors can get by on word-of-mouth, but the vast majority of new and somewhat established authors have to rely on solid marketing practices, which include making your book visually appealing. That's where your book's aesthetics need to be visually compelling and professional.

Enter the book cover.

Some readers rely on recommendations and other readers simply see an excellent cover and will buy with no hesitation. Sadly, if you're a new or relatively unknown author, simply relying on referrals isn't enough. Even though a great cover design can seal the deal with some browsing customers, it's only going to make up a fraction of your sales.

Enter the book description.

Your description is what should entice browsing customers into buying your book now, not later. The words you use need to resonate with your potential reader in a way that makes them feel they cannot miss out on reading your story.

Executing these elements will take time and adjustments before you get it right, so let's look at the three separate parts. When you go to launch your book, these three elements need to be firmly in place with a little bit of flexibility.

KEYWORDS, COVER & COPY

When laying the groundwork for your book launch, think of these three items: keywords, cover, and copy. Without focusing on these three elements, you risk launching your book recklessly and relying solely on luck. Does this require months of research? No, but you may have to put in a few hours of work refining, tweaking, and perfecting what you have.

Start with selecting the right keywords so you increase your book's likeliness of discovery and validate customer search queries. Without having the proper keywords in place, you're going to have to do a lot more promotion just to get any attention. Whereas, having the right keywords selected ahead of time gives your publication a small boost in organic discoverability. Once Amazon delivers your book to the right audience, and as long as you have the other two elements set up—great cover and ad copy—the rest should be a straightforward choice for browsing customers.

KEYWORD RESEARCH & SELECTION

After you launch your book, you can place keywords in nearly every digital nook and cranny of your publication. Rather than complicate the process with what keywords go where, build a list of keywords first. Selecting the right keywords comes down to a few simple steps.

First, describe your book or elements of your book in a phrase comprising two or more words. Put yourself in the mind of your ideal reader. Determine what that customer is searching for so you can find the keywords that will allow them to stumble over your book.

Next, build a list of one to two dozen keyword phrases. Don't worry about prioritizing any one keyword, since you'll sort that out later.

Last, confirm customers are searching for each keyword phrase on Amazon.

Let's break down the full process and give you practical steps for researching and selecting the right keywords.

Install the free browser extension, KIP Scout, a tool that helps provide relevant product details on Amazon (US). This tool helps give you all the relevant details about a publication brought up in a search query. Normally, you'd have to visit every book's product page to get an accurate idea of how it's performing in the marketplace. With KIP Scout, you see it all with a click or two. Normally, if you visit every page, you'll scroll to the **Product Details** section, located halfway down the page, where it displays the following information.

ASIN

Also known as the Amazon Standard Identification Number, this ten-character code is what Amazon assigns your product for listing on their site. The ASIN is inessential for anything in your research; it's merely an identifier on Amazon's marketplace.

PUBLISHER

The publisher's name, also known as the publishing imprint, appears here. Most times when authors publish through Kindle Direct Publishing, they're assigned the imprint name of "Independently Published." This usually means they don't have a publishing imprint or are using Amazon's free-assigned ISBN. At the time of this writing, you can put any name in this field to replace the default imprint name KDP assigns your ebooks, but not for print books. Otherwise, you'll need to come with your own ISBN if you want another imprint name in this field for both paperback and hardcover books.

PUBLICATION DATE

This info is pertinent in knowing the recency of the title. If the book published years ago still sells regularly, it's probably a perennial seller. You'll find the publication date occasionally in the search results just below the book's title. If there isn't too much metadata taking up the space below the title, you'll see the publication date at the end of the second-line text.

MISCELLANEOUS

Other options include: Language, Text-to-Speech, Screen Reader, Enhanced Typesetting, X-Ray, Word Wise, Sticky notes, File Size/Print Length. Though having this information will not make or break the success of your book, it'll certainly give you small clues of what you should include in your publication. These sections highlight customer expectations, so if you find a successful title in your book's category, consider applying similar strategies to your own.

BEST SELLERS RANK

Pay close attention to this section. Thankfully, KIP Scout provides the Best Sellers Rank at a glance. When you search for a keyword phrase on Amazon, the website typically displays around sixteen products on the first page when you use the "Sort by: Featured" filter. Without the extension, you would need to click on each product, scroll halfway down the page to view the ABSR, and then return to the search results. You'd have to repeat this process for all sixteen titles to get their current ABSR. With the extension, you can see the current ABSR, the price, estimated monthly sales, estimated monthly revenue, number of reviews, page count, and profitability all in one place.

CUSTOMER REVIEWS

Amazon strongly recommends having at least fifteen reviews with an average rating of three-and-a-half stars or higher for your book to be considered retail-ready. Without this minimum, your book is at a higher risk of being buried on the website, while other titles with the recommended review count have a better chance of standing out. I'll share more information about reviews in the chapter about building an advanced reader copy team.

Now that we've covered the details of the **Product Details** section, let's focus on the practical steps of researching and selecting the right keywords for your book.

When using KIP Scout in your research, you're only needing it for a snapshot of how a title is performing with a keyword in search. The ABSR shows proof of concept. Should enough titles show a great rank under a keyword, it means customers are actively buying content from the keyword search.

Once you have KIP Scout installed, you'll need to enable it for incognito mode under the **Settings** for **Extensions** in your browser. Otherwise, it won't work for how you will use it. This extension is only good for the Amazon US, UK, and Canada Marketplaces (with plans to expand to other regions), so if you're doing research on other regional marketplaces, you'll have to click on every product served in your research and scroll to the **Product Details** for the relevant info.

Open your internet browser in incognito mode, so Amazon serves you the most general keywords and products. In a normal browser, Amazon will serve keywords and products based on *your* previous browsing and buying history. You aren't selecting keywords for *you*, but for the public. Opening incognito mode is like starting with a blank slate, so you get the cleanest results possible.

Now comes the fun part! Take your list of keyword phrases and begin typing them into the Amazon search window for the **Kindle Store** or **Books** options in the dropdown. Type one word at a time and stop for Amazon to autosuggest popular keyword phrases associated with that word. Jot down any keywords you feel fit your title best, then continue typing out the rest of your original keyword phrase.

Once you've spent enough time on one keyword variation, you can go back and try substituting other letters of the alphabet to uncover hidden gems. For instance, if the first keyword in my phrase was "workout" I would hit the spacebar, then type the letter "a" to see what Amazon autosuggests. Once that's done, I do "workout b" to see what it brings up, then "c" and "d" and so on.

Be selective with the keyword phrases you put on your list. When in doubt, toss it out. Never sacrifice quality selections for the sake of profit. The keyword phrases you should use are what best suit your book, not what best lines your wallet. Yes, profit is important, but that'll fall in line if your book is the right fit.

I stress caution when selecting keywords that have perceived relevance to your title. When you assign keywords to your book, you're essentially telling the Amazon search engine, "Hey, trust me. This is what my book is about."

If Amazon serves your product to browsing customers with a keyword that doesn't convert to sales, you erode digital trust—also known as relevance. You don't just want high relevance for the keywords you choose—you need it. Building relevance requires the right mix of keywords, a strong cover, and compelling marketing copy, ensuring potential customers buy whenever they see your product.

That's what Amazon wants most—to make money—and they can only do that if their customers are happily finding what they need on the platform with as little friction as possible. When you select the wrong keywords or irrelevant phrases, the wrong customer gets served your book and doesn't buy. That's not good. After all, Amazon needs to keep the customer happy, and by selecting the wrong keyword, you've just hindered that mission.

Once you have a full list of keyword phrases, it's time to search each phrase you curated. Type the keyword phrase into the Search Bar, then hit Enter.

Take a quick glance at the product volume range in the top left corner. It'll say something like "1-16 of over 50,000 results." These results represent products associated with the keyword phrase. Higher volume means more competition, while lower numbers indicate less competition. Authors should aim for keywords with low competition but high demand, as they offer the best chance of visibility without getting lost in a sea of more popular terms.

The product volume won't make any bit of difference though if no one is buying the products related to the keyword phrase. Sure, a keyword can have a hundred or fewer products attached to it, but if the books have a poor ABSR, this shows there's no competition and no audience.

That's why you audit the overall average ABSR of the books served on this page. When you see a book in your niche that ranks well, investigate it more by visiting the product page. Focus on the bestseller rank while noting any relevant placement categories assigned to each title. Also, ask yourself, "Does my book fit in?"

Although you might believe your book relates to a keyword term, the general population might disagree based on their purchasing behavior. For example, I might have a book about full-body stretching. If I type "stretching" and all it serves back to me are erotica books, then I probably don't want to use that keyword.

Once you've identified a keyword phrase and the right search results for your niche, you'll need to gather the ABSR of every product while excluding any Sponsored Product Ads (designated by a Sponsored tag).

I aim for an ABSR range between 10,000 and 100,000, which usually corresponds to about one to fifteen book sales per day. With the right marketing and promotion, most authors can hit these numbers. If the ABSR drops to between 1 and 10,000, you're up against heavy competition, with those books likely selling between fifteen and over six thousand copies per day. Any rank above 100,000 suggests a book that might only sell a copy every other day—or even less often.

The reason you're focused on the first-page search results is to see if you have a dog in the fight for a specific keyword. Getting your title listed on the first-page search will increase the likelihood of a customer buying. The farther down your title is in search results, the less likely a customer will find your title.

However—and this is a significant point—every Amazon customer sees personalized search results based on their browsing and buying history. While you might find great keywords for your title and build keyword relevance through sales, it doesn't mean you'll get first-page placement every time, especially with incognito mode. The whole point of putting together a curated keywords list isn't to always appear everywhere, every time. You're simply training Amazon's search engine to serve your title to the right customer at the right time.

Once you launch your book, don't bother seeing if your title appears in search for all your selected keywords. Spend that time writing your next book or promoting your current book. Nothing builds relevance, like cold, hard sales. Make that happen, and Amazon will happily send you the traffic. Visiting search results to see if your title comes up is a needless vanity pursuit, so don't waste your time checking.

As you sift through your list of keywords, place an asterisk next to the keywords you feel the strongest about and also note any phrases with similar words or overlap. Your list should narrow down to about one to two dozen. Be especially discerning about the keywords you select. By now, you've compiled a broad list, but you're refining it with more informed, algorithm-based selections.

> Fun fact: *The long-tail keyword—a phrase of three words or more—hyper-focuses on one audience instead of more generalized content with a shorter keyword phrase. For example, "home fitness" describes a massive audience, whereas "home fitness for men over 55" narrows down to a specific audience.*

KDP allows for seven backend keyword slots, which help with your book's discoverability on the Amazon marketplace. These slots are for keyword phrases that aren't visible to customers but are used by Amazon's search algorithms to categorize your book. Avoid cramming too many keywords into a single slot when you publish your title. Also, be calculated and meticulous about record-keeping—track every keyword phrase you use.

CHAPTER 2: LAYING THE GROUNDWORK

As a general example, here's a list of related keywords I'm using for a book I'm doing keyword research for:

1. home fitness
2. home workout
3. workout plan

KDP allows authors up to fifty characters per keyword slot, with seven slots available. You won't need to include commas or dashes since they'll simply ignore them. Use every character in a slot wisely. For the previous example, you could combine those related keyword phrases into one slot:

home fitness workout plan

Amazon will sort out broad matches from your selected keywords, essentially those individual keyword choices I mentioned before. When I'm researching keywords, I'll create a master list that I can refer to later when I'm needing to update my title with more current and relevant keywords. My list would look like this:

1. home fitness workout plan
    a. home fitness
    b. home workout
    c. workout plan

A few years ago, Dave Chesson and the team at Kindlepreneur ran a case study on using the seven backend keywords.[viii] They discovered that having a healthy mix of exact keyword choices and combined keywords increased the likelihood of discovery on Amazon. Meaning, a few backend keyword slots should include an uncombined keyword—or exact keyword—and a few slots should have combined keywords. Your keyword selection needs to be diverse, painting a picture of what readers can expect in your book.

As your original list breaks down into the seven compartmentalized keywords, you'll have each keyword to use in other areas including the title, subtitle, series name, description, A+ Content, the editorial reviews section of your book, and your book-specific bio.

Nonfiction authors have an advantage over fiction authors in being able to create a title filled with keywords. Yes, some fiction authors can get away with keyword use in their title, subtitle or series name, but fiction readers have a different mindset than nonfiction readers. For nonfiction, the readers are searching for a solution to their problem. If you can organically weave keywords into your title, subtitle or series name, all the better, but avoid going overboard. Your title shouldn't be so long that it's hard for you to remember the name or you get your full title truncated on Amazon.

Search engine algorithms are very sensitive to keyword overuse and abuse. While some sellers may get away with stuffing their product listings with keywords, Amazon can and will suppress those listings or even remove a book if the subtitle isn't on the cover or if the listing violates their guidelines. When selecting keywords for your title, subtitle, and series name, aim for quality over quantity. Use one or two carefully chosen keywords per title, subtitle, and series name to ensure you're not overstuffing, while still making your book discoverable.

Note: You do not need a series name to publish on KDP.

Now that you have your basic title, subtitle, series name, and seven backend keywords, let's expand on keyword use by incorporating them into key areas, starting with the book description. Including keywords in your description helps improve discoverability and supports customer validation. The system indexes the keywords in a word cloud to assist with search and organization, while customers who land on your book's product page will recognize familiar terms from their search, reinforcing their choice.

Another high-value area for slipping in your keywords includes the A+ Content. This option is only available after you launch a book or an ebook pre-order. You need to first have the product page before Amazon can add a special section called **From the Publisher**. In this section, you're able to share images, comparisons, charts, and other marketing materials in five compartments—also known as modules.

The Amazon Advertising Certification Courses explain that combining image-based and text-based modules yields the best results for search engine optimization. For each image, you're allowed up to 100 characters. I experimented by using the same combined keywords from KDP's seven backend keywords in my A+ Content. Unfortunately, the A+ Content moderators didn't approve them and simply referred me to their guidelines. To avoid this, I now limit the keyword slot to just one relevant keyword to stay within the guidelines and prevent disapproval.

A lot of authors are nailing it with A+ Content, creating beautiful graphics that are sure to influence a browsing customer to buy. However, limiting yourself to only images leaves behind a lot of customers who could be influenced by text-based modules. The savvy author will leverage every marketing opportunity through A+ Content while search engine optimizing it for better discoverability.

To access the other options for discoverability, you will need to create an Amazon Author Profile through Author Central, a free-to-use marketing tool for sharing all things related to your author brand. You get your author bio, author profile picture, and your listed books all in one place.

When crafting your author bio, view it as a way to enhance your book's discoverability. Use two to three brief paragraphs to introduce who you are, what you write, and any other relevant interests. Including a few relevant keywords helps make your listing easier to find. While making your product listing more discoverable won't directly affect your rank, it increases the likelihood of a sale. More traffic to your product page means more potential buyers, boosting your chances of success.

Amazon Author Central allows you to claim any title you've published and adds the option for editorial reviews (available in the US only). You can add snippets from reviews you receive from external sources but be sure to credit the source. Avoid using reviews already featured on your book's product page, as it will be redundant. You'll get bonus points if you can include a keyword in your editorial review snippet, but don't force it. Remember, you also have additional opportunities for keyword placement in these sections

- From the Author
- From the Inside Flap
- From the Back Cover
- About the Author

Each section is another opportunity to include a keyword but only fill out the fields if they're relevant to your title. For example, if you don't have any unique back cover text or an inside flap (typically found on hardcover editions with dust jackets), you should leave those sections blank. One section I like to take advantage of is "About the Author." While you already have a bio on your main author profile, this section is different. It allows you to create a bio that's unique to that particular book. Share something specific about you that connects to the book. This bio should be more focused and intentional, while your main author bio can be broader.

You can use keywords in more places than just within your KDP dashboard. These keywords help make your book more discoverable, especially as you drive more sales and increase relevance for the keywords you've chosen. While it's important to use them strategically in your book listing, think of keywords as tools that work across multiple areas to attract the right readers.

For a deeper dive into how keywords function on the Amazon Marketplace, check out my five-time award-winning book *Amazon Keywords for Books*, available at every major online retailer and library system. But don't feel pressured to stop reading now and pick up that book. We're focused on planning your bestselling book launch here. Once you have a roadmap for your launch, that book will serve as a valuable resource for diving deeper into keywords.

CREATING THE COPY

Copywriting is the act of writing text intended to persuade people to take a particular action. If you have the budget and aren't sure where to begin, you can hire a professional to write your book description. For example, I've worked with Brian Meeks, author of *Mastering Amazon Descriptions*, to write my book descriptions. While I've published many books without a copywriter, I found that outsourcing this task allowed me to focus on other important aspects of my business.

If you want to craft your own book description, follow these basic rules:

1. Avoid unnecessary details. A book description isn't a summary of the book or a place to showcase sample writing. Don't get lost in details or family trees—focus on the key selling points and what makes the book compelling to readers. Keep it concise and impactful, highlighting the unique value of your book.
2. Don't write from the author's point of view. Avoid phrasing like "You should read my book" or "Let me show you what you can expect." Instead, focus on what the book offers readers and how it benefits them. Authors should study bestselling books in their niche to determine the best point of view, as this can vary.
3. The key to a compelling book description is creating curiosity, not giving everything away upfront. Skip mentioning characters and events that are inessential to the main plotline. For nonfiction, create intrigue by withholding key details—don't give away the value for free. Instead of saying, "Did you know you can lose 10 pounds by limiting your food intake and exercising thirty minutes a day?" try, "Discover the secret to losing ten pounds safely in the next month."

4. Limit your text to what you need, nothing more. You should get your point across in 150 words or fewer.
5. Don't use wordy language; it'll just confuse most folks who are looking for a quick overview of your book.

Every book description can follow a simple formula. Let's take each piece one at a time.

Start with a powerful hook that clearly states the pain point for nonfiction or the conflict for fiction. Craft it to quickly capture attention, making it short, punchy, and easy to read at a glance. The goal of marketing copy is to get browsing customers to read the entire description. Most will leave the page if they see a dense block of text. Break it up into bite-sized pieces to encourage them to click the "Read More" link.

Next, describe the book's genre and target audience. Organically weave keywords from your list into your description for search engine optimization and customer validation. Integrating relevant terms in nonfiction books is relatively easy because most long-tail phrases read like a complete thought or fit naturally into a sentence. For fiction, using keywords meaningfully becomes harder. Is it impossible? No, but it's going to be a challenge.

Now, showcase elements of the story arc or subject matter. You'll want to avoid spoilers or basic summaries. The copy you write needs to be compelling and create a sense of intrigue. Lead the customers through an exciting array of elements showcased in your book, but leave out the granular details they'll find in the content.

The last two elements tie closely together in highlighting your book's unique selling point and ending with a call-to-action. You can see these items in my book description for *Amazon Keywords for Books*:

> You'll love this comprehensive book on keywords, because it's easy to follow and will teach you what you need to forever master the subject.
>
> Get it now.

I shared how and why they'll enjoy my book in the first sentence. Then, wrapped it all up with three simple words: Get it now. Don't overthink that last line. I used to subscribe to the belief that you had to tell customers exactly what to do, like:

> Scroll up and hit the Buy Now button to get the very best insights for keyword mastery.

Sadly, this text reads like you're talking down to the customer, as if they're not already intimately familiar with how to shop on Amazon. Most everyone is familiar with online shopping these days, so they really don't need the mini-tutorial on how to check out. Will any customer take umbrage at that? Probably not, but I won't take any chances.

Besides, why say something in seventeen words what you can say in three? Keep it super simple. This goes back to the less is more philosophy used in the hook. Create text that's easy to read at a glance, breaking information into bite-sized chunks. This allows browsing customers to easily read from top to bottom and make their decision—to buy or not to buy.

One way to create a book description without all the fuss is through artificial intelligence (AI) tools like ChatGPT or even one of my

CHAPTER 2: LAYING THE GROUNDWORK

favorite writing tools, Dibbly Create. I wish I'd had these kinds of tools back in 2014! Draft a book description the best you can, then share it with AI. I'll give AI a prompt with the previously mentioned guidelines and request it to use any keywords from my master list. You may not get a perfect description on the first try, so be persistent and guide AI with some patience. Once you get the right sequence of questions and requests put together in your prompts, save it. When you go back to update your book description or generate a new one, you have all the prompts to get you cranking out killer copy in minutes.

When you have a book description drafted, submit it to a few peers for some feedback. Have them identify structural issues, typos, grammatical errors, or areas to abbreviate or expand. I've found most authors tend to go a little long, writing sentences that span across three to five lines. That's just far too long and can seem cumbersome to most browsing customers, especially if they're viewing the copy on a mobile device. Your job is to make it easy for the customer to understand the general premise of your book as quickly as possible, so they can decide whether to buy or not.

I recommend finding authors within your niche so you get honest feedback from people representative of your target audience. While you can still work with other authors, you'll find getting an author experienced in your niche will help you craft better copy. Between Facebook Groups, forums, and other areas of social media, you'll find three or more authors willing to give you a few minutes of their time.

I've got an entire channel in my Discord community dedicated to book description feedback, so if you're lacking any peers to review your book description, pop into <u>DaleLinks.com/Discord</u>. You always have the choice to disagree with feedback, but I highly recommend you keep it to yourself, since most folks are volunteering their time. If you need more context or clarification, just ask.

I highly recommend three excellent books about writing better book descriptions:

1. *Mastering Amazon Descriptions* by Brian Meeks
2. *How to Write a Sizzling Synopsis* by Bryan Cohen
3. *Sales Copy Unleashed* by Robert Ryan

Getting insights and tips from these experts will certainly sharpen your skills.

CREATING THE COVER

Everyone judges a book by its cover, with few exceptions to the rule. Yes, if you're an established author—like Stephen King or JK Rowling—you have the luxury of publishing a book with a shoddy cover. (Although I doubt their publishers would allow that.) Most longtime readers will skip over a bad book cover from a new-to-them author in favor of reading the next big release from their favorite author. Having a modest following or no readership at all puts you at a greater disadvantage than those established authors. Sure, some readers might recommend your book to other readers, but it's hard to even convince that one reader to read your book with a less than professional book cover.

Let's address the elephant in the room: do-it-yourself book covers. Most author-created covers end up looking unprofessional or poorly designed, which can make potential readers question the quality of the book inside. A subpar cover often gives the impression of a rushed or low-quality product, leading to fewer sales and attracting fewer readers. While there are some exceptions, authors should generally avoid creating their own covers to ensure their book makes the right first impression.

Sure, if you have experience in graphic design and know how to draft a cover design in line with the niche, then you're good to go. The rest of us must rely on professional cover designers. No, you don't want just any old graphic designer for the job. You specifically need an experienced professional who has a portfolio of completed projects and client testimonials.

The part that holds many indie authors back from investing in a quality cover design is the expense—or the perception of how much it might cost. I've seen covers ranging from $5 to $1,200, and I'm confident you can find excellent designs at any price point. I've even surprised viewers on my YouTube channel with cover design case studies. While higher-priced designs often stand out, you can find high-quality, professional options at any budget.

To see my recommendations for quality cover designers, refer to the Resources section. I used and vetted my cover designers, so those I recommend are those I share based on my honest experience. However, do your research, because there are quite a few other options outside the ones on my list.

For authors who truly can't afford to hire a cover designer, I suggest *DIY Book Covers* by Derek Murphy. It's a course showing authors how to create their own covers using, of all things, Microsoft Word to create a design. While I'd rather see authors hiring out, I totally understand it's not an option for everyone. Derek has extensive experience in drafting killer cover designs and coaching authors, so you're in very capable hands.

The best part? He doesn't charge a dime for his expertise, and I've never seen him try to upsell customers. Even if he did, Derek works hard delivering premium quality content for no money in exchange. You won't find anyone with a bigger heart for this business than him.

If you have the budget (or time, if you're DIY), create at least one to three cover variations and get feedback from readers and other authors. Yes, you should trust your cover designer, but even the best professionals might miss one minor detail, font choice, or layout. Getting another set of eyes on the design will help identify the most effective cover and will show you how to improve it.

Having a few cover design variations will also help later on. When book sales drop, consider switching out the cover design for a different variation. This'll keep your book's product page fresh and browsing customers more interested in checking out your book. Even traditionally published books get a facelift now and then. Self-published books are no different.

EVALUATING PERFORMANCE

Knowing that the success of your book relies on three key elements—keywords, copy, and cover—how will you know if they're working? Sales are an obvious indicator, but remember, tracking success also means evaluating visibility, engagement, and the effectiveness of your marketing efforts. The ultimate goal is not just sales but sustained growth and reach.

Of course, success also depends on a solid marketing and promotional strategy. You can't rely on keywords, copy, and cover alone to drive traffic. To gain Amazon's virtual trust, you must prove your book is relevant and has the potential to generate sales. Without this, Amazon won't prioritize your book across their marketplace.

If you're marketing and promoting your book with regularity and you still don't see sales, you'll know you have a problem with your keywords, cover, and copy. Far too many authors get it wrong when they blame Amazon for the lack of sales. All Amazon does is provide a place for you to sell your book. The platform relies heavily on a machine-based algorithm, but you can't hack the search engine without generating more sales.

Before you lose your cool and blame Amazon, take a step back and re-analyze your keywords, cover, and copy. If things aren't working after your launch, go back and adjust these three elements. I implore you to take your time, perfect them, get feedback, then adjust accordingly.

For all the preparation in the world, you might still need to adjust these elements later. The process will be the same whether you're preparing to launch your book or are updating an already launched book.

Though I've mentioned peer review as an option, it's worth emphasizing again: no author should try to figure out their entire business alone. Reaching out to your network for help puts you at a greater advantage than those who struggle on their own. As authors, we often work in isolation. While our intuition can guide many aspects of our business, relying solely on it can create a narrow, biased perspective.

Finding other authors to work with is easier in theory than in practice. Start with where you are—anyone you know, whether in person or online. Authors who write in the same niche can be more helpful, but you shouldn't limit yourself to just those in your exact niche. Even working with authors in a related field can provide valuable feedback, and you'll gain insights tailored to a similar audience.

Be prepared to get advice you might or might not agree with. Yes, it sucks when someone tells you your book cover is trash, your keywords are wrong, and your book description wouldn't draw flies if it was written in dung, much less a few meager sales. As with everything in life, take the advice with a pinch of salt. When you need a better understanding of where someone is coming from, ask. Avoid being defensive or argumentative. That's a surefire way of getting no additional help when you need it.

However, you shouldn't entirely dismiss feedback, because every bit can help in some capacity. I once heard someone say, "If one person calls you a horse, they're crazy. If three people say it, it's a conspiracy. But if ten people say it, it's time to saddle up!"

Though I've given you one resource for connecting with other authors, it's not the only option. Consider other social platforms like Facebook, Reddit, X (fka Twitter), Instagram, and YouTube. Stick with one platform rather than spreading yourself too thin across all platforms. You'll build more meaningful and longer lasting relationships when you're present in one space rather than split in a dozen different ones.

Yes, I realize connecting with other people might be a tall ask for the introverts out there, but you're only a few keystrokes and mouse clicks away from connecting. Don't let that be the one boundary keeping you away from invaluable feedback your book needs before its launch.

ANALYZING KEYWORDS, COVER, & COPY WITH AMAZON ADS

Amazon Advertising is an invaluable tool for assessing product viability, but only if authors analyze the data. Rather than go into great detail about how to leverage the platform, I'll review the indicators of what is or isn't working in your published book.

Though Amazon Ads won't serve your book any good pre-launch, you can still use it later, after your book is on the market and has a few reviews. In the Amazon Advertising Certification Courses, they shared how products are more apt to sell when they're retail-ready. This includes having an enticing product description, great product images, and at least fifteen reviews with an average of 3.5 stars or greater. You'll learn more about getting book reviews in the next chapter, so hang tight—we'll get that dialed in soon.

When you run Amazon ads, sales confirm that your cover and copy work effectively. Let me get a little more specific about how you'll know.

When your ad is getting tons of impressions and no clicks, you need to consider two very important elements: the targeting and your cover. First, determine if your targeting is off-base or irrelevant to your book. You'll know this based on what you find in your **Search Terms** report or in the manual targeting you selected. To check for relevance, search for that keyword or product on Amazon. When presented with the search results, scroll through it and determine if your book fits with the rest.

While I'd like to think every target I choose for a manual campaign is relevant to my book, the majority of Amazon customers may think otherwise. Pay attention to customer behavior; their actions often reveal what works for them, and sometimes, that means your book isn't the right fit.

Assuming your targeting is on point and fully relevant, what do you do if you're not getting any clicks along with your impressions? Perhaps your cover design isn't enticing enough for browsing customers to click on your ad. Another possibility is that the ad copy isn't compelling, or maybe the audience isn't right for your book. One reason I believe Amazon Advertising isn't for everyone is that some authors refuse to analyze the data. Instead of looking for what isn't working and adjusting accordingly, they dismiss the platform altogether, claiming it doesn't work.

Oh, it works alright. Just not with what you have right now. Given time and consistently monitoring your analytics, you'll be able to improve sales with your ads.

If an ad is driving a ton of clicks with no sales, you probably have a marketing copy issue—assuming, of course, that your targeting is relevant. A click means your cover and title are compelling enough to get customers to visit the product page.

It's better to discover your cover needs improvement while getting impressions, not after you start paying for clicks. Once you start getting clicks, you're being charged, and you need those clicks to convert into sales to avoid losing money. Scrutinize every element of your book and ad campaign. A click shows that a customer considers your product worth investigating further.

That's where your book description plays a critical role. If it isn't compelling, no beautiful cover will be enough to drive sales. Sure, you might get a few people who buy based on your cover or recommendations, but most Amazon traffic comes from shoppers who don't know you yet. They need a compelling reason to buy and read your book in order to convert into a sale.

Of course, once you've got an ad running that converts clicks into sales more often, you can assume your book cover and copy are effective.

One last tip when using Amazon Advertising is to leverage research and discovery ads. Set up an automated targeting campaign with a budget you can afford and let it run on a book for a few months. Then, review the monthly report from the Search Terms tab in your Amazon Ads dashboard to identify high-converting targets and eliminate irrelevant ones. Focus especially on the keywords and products that generate sales.

Automated targeting campaigns will reveal what keywords convert the best for your book. This means if you're ever indecisive about what keywords to use for your book, Amazon Ads will give you the answer.

The high-converting keywords might be something worth considering for your backend in your book's metadata. Remember, you'll want to avoid any trademarks, author names, titles, and Amazon-related terms in your seven backend keywords. Yes, you can use those options for targeting in an Amazon Ad, but you can't use them elsewhere.

Once a year, it's a good idea to sift through your **Search Terms** report for the year and consider switching out older keyword phrases that might not have as much traction. Avoid changing your words more than every three months to one year because you might confuse the Amazon algorithms and limit the reach of your book.

The three fundamental elements—keywords, cover, and copy—can feel abstract at first, and if you're new to the business, they can be overwhelming. You'll only get answers after preparing before your book launch to test your ideas or after the book is launched. No author should expect immediate results from minor changes. As with any business, driving more sales requires trial and error, along with patience and a willingness to learn.

You can't rely solely on your product being perfect. Instead, you need to dedicate extra time to perfecting those three key elements to improve your chances of success with your book launch. While perfection isn't expected, you should strive to get as close to it as possible given your skill set, connections, and available resources.

CHAPTER 3:
BUILD AN ARC TEAM

A critical element to any book launch's success is the advance reader team—also known as an ARC team. This team consists of readers willing to read a copy of your book ahead of the release and leave an honest review on any major online retailer or book site. Having social proof helps in converting more browsing customers into buyers, so you need to load up your book with as many reviews as possible to make it happen.

The Amazon Advertising Certification Course shared that 91% of customers visit the reviews before making a purchase. Over nine out of ten people will search for reviews on your product and if you lack sufficient social proof, most customers will leave to consider another product *with* feedback.

To be clear, you can still successfully publish a book without reviews on it, but you're at a greater disadvantage over established products with reviews. Nothing attracts a crowd like a crowd. Bringing your own crowd will help with just that.

The vast majority of newbie authors believe it's impossible to start an ARC team since they don't have followers. While that is true to a certain extent, it doesn't have to be for you. Having a following helps but isn't mandatory to acquire a solid ARC team.

Building your ARC team will take time, and it's important to manage expectations. Not everyone on your team will leave a review. Life happens, and some readers may not finish the book or may forget to leave a review altogether. But with persistence, you'll grow your team, and as you continue building your author platform, those reviews will come.

In fact, in my five-time award-winning book *Amazon Reviews for Books*, I mention that, on average, a third of all readers will leave a review on or after launch day. Readers often have the best intentions, but life often gets in the way. Many people find that reading and reviewing a book is harder than they initially expected. Others may simply forget to leave a review once the excitement of finishing the book fades.

Some authors have a better conversion of readers to reviewers, but generally, three out of ten readers will actually leave a review. A few best practices in place will help increase that conversion, but let's start with the basics and progress to how you're going to increase that conversion rate.

ARC TEAM MANAGEMENT SYSTEMS

In my second year publishing fitness books, I accidentally stumbled into the process of building an advanced reader copy team. I knew how valuable reviews could be, so when I was preparing to launch another title, I contacted my email newsletter subscribers. The request was simple: Would anyone be interested in receiving advance access

CHAPTER 3: BUILD AN ARC TEAM

to my upcoming book for an honest review posted on Amazon on or after launch day?

I wish I could share that I had an enormous email list, but I don't think it was ever over a couple thousand, and even then, only 35% of my email subscribers actually opened their emails. That small window of opportunity was enough to get me a few willing readers. Sadly, that modest turnout didn't bring in many reviews on launch day, but as you'll come to understand, *something* is better than nothing.

Every author should at least shoot for one review on launch day and no, you shouldn't post a review for yourself and, as we'll later cover, avoid encouraging your close friends and family to leave reviews.

Back when I started my first ARC team, I relied on a rather archaic yet effective system. The process was simple:

1. Reach out to readers through my email newsletter and social media.
2. Track ARC readers or segment them in my email newsletter system.
3. Send advanced access to readers at least one month before the book launch.
4. Follow up with readers on the book launch.
5. Follow up with readers who hadn't posted a review two weeks after the book launch.

This system still works today, so you truly don't need anything complex. You'll notice I didn't include groveling or pestering readers for reviews. That's because you'll only soil your reputation and seem needy.

Now, many online services cover all aspects of an ARC team—whether you're looking to drive the traffic or allow the site to drive traffic for you. Not to mention, these sites help manage ebook distribution and notifications to readers, leaving you to do whatever else you need in your business. That means you can skip the two-week post-launch reminder, because those sites will cover it for you.

DO-IT-YOURSELF ARC TEAM MANAGEMENT

First, you'll need an email marketing service to manage your email list while staying compliant with online laws and regulations. Don't use your personal email to communicate with your ARC team, as doing so could land you in spam folders or, worse, get your email address flagged by providers. Besides being time-consuming, it could also put you at risk of legal issues. Using a dedicated email marketing service streamlines the process, allowing you to focus more on your writing or promoting your upcoming book launch.

Look into MailerLite, Mailchimp, or any email marketing service provider that best aligns with your budget. I'm partial to MailerLite and have used it with great success for years. At the time of this writing, MailerLite offers free access for up to 1,000 subscribers without any additional fees or restrictions. By the time you hit that threshold, you should earn enough to invest in the upgrade. If not, cull the herd by deleting inactive subscribers. List-churn happens, so you'll need to remove email subscribers who are no longer interested in opening your emails.

I'm sure they won't mind if you delete their name, freeing up that slot for a reader actively invested in your author brand. I can think of countless times I've subscribed to an email newsletter, only to unsubscribe later when I no longer needed it. I can always resubscribe when my situation changes and I require the newsletter again.

Getting readers to sign up for a newsletter can be a pain, but it's certainly worth the effort, especially when managing your own ARC team. The first line of defense when looking for ARC readers is often your own subscribers. For published authors, simply include a call-to-action at the beginning and end of your book, offering readers exclusive advance access. Raving fans and avid readers will love saving a few bucks they'd otherwise spend on your book while helping ensure the success of your book launch. Even if you haven't published a book yet, include this call-to-action in your next publication.

The key to managing an email list, especially an ARC list, is full transparency and consistent messaging. For me, that means keeping readers informed about what's happening and what's coming up for the upcoming book launch. I treat my ARC list differently from my regular lists to maintain that trust. When a reader joins my ARC team, I focus on delivering value and building trust, ensuring I don't undermine it by straying from the list's original purpose.

Even if I have an incredible deal or product launch outside of my books, I don't bother my ARC team with those promotions. If they want updates about special deals, sales, or anything not related to advance reader copies, they'll need to join a separate mailing list for that content. It's essential to keep your ARC list focused, so when subscribers sign up, make it clear they're joining the ARC Team. I always let people know exactly what they're signing up for with clear sign-up options, so they'll know whether they're on the ARC list or another list.

Delivering your advance reader copies is tricky and raises valid concerns about cost. It shouldn't cost you a dime to hand out ebook copies of your upcoming release. You can send a print copy to your ARC team members, but avoid doing it unless you absolutely must shoulder the expense. Getting print proofs—also known as author copies on KDP—can be costly, especially having to pay for shipping twice.

For instance, you can buy wholesale copies of your book to be sent to your house. That shipment is going to cost a pretty penny, even if you order in bulk. Then, you'll have to mail that book from you to the ARC reader, with packing materials and shipping costing more. You'll still have to account for the time and energy you put into fulfilling distribution.

Rather than send print copies, save your budget and send out digital copies only. Earlier in my career, I used Google Drive to deliver a zipped file with three versions of my ebook: epub, mobi, and PDF. In the zipped folder, I provided instructions on how to load the ARC into their preferred reading devices. These days, mobi files are inessential and antiquated. Stick with sending the PDF or epub version of your ebook.

Here's a simple Read Me file with loading instructions you can include with your zipped file:

> AUTHOR'S NOTE
>
> Hey, thanks so much for joining my Advance Reader Copy team for [Insert Your Book Here]. To load the ebook to your ereader, visit Amazon.com/SendToKindle. The epub file will give you the ability to adjust the font size and type, while the PDF comes

> with a fixed layout where you can only zoom in on the text and cannot alter it.
>
> All the best,
>
> Dale L. Roberts

Use the previous message to explain how to load an ebook to a Kindle ereader. Remove any friction that'll prevent your team members from reading your book; this includes showing them something they could otherwise Google search. The less work they have to do, the more apt they will be to leave a review upon launch.

DIY TRACKING ARC READERS

Google Sheets is a great, free resource to track reviews. When a reader posts a review, you can jot it down in the spreadsheet. You will see who did and didn't follow-up on their end of the deal. When a reader hasn't left a review on a book after one reminder, I remove them from all future ARC Teams.

For now, you simply have to trust your ARC readers will read the book and leave an honest review on Amazon. You can continue prospecting for more ARC Team members through your newsletter, website, book, or social media. As long as you keep adding new readers to the team, you'll never run out of people to support your launch.

Distribute copies in advance based on your book's length and the reader's availability. For instance, a dense textbook will likely need three months for a reader to complete, while a short story could be read in a day. As a general guideline, give your ARC readers two to four weeks to read and review your book. For longer works like epic novels or extensive nonfiction, you might need to provide more time. Ultimately, you'll have to determine the best time frame based on the type of book and your audience's needs.

If your readers miss the launch date and post reviews a bit later, that's okay. While it's ideal to have reviews come in at launch, receiving them afterward is still better than getting no reviews at all. Even delayed reviews contribute to your book's credibility and visibility in the long run.

Having a consistent flow of reviews can have a positive effect on product sales. One theory is that recency of reviews aids in relevance on the Amazon platform. I'm not sure about the validity of this theory, but we can all agree that having a steadily growing supply of reviews will help convert browsing customers into buyers.

Your ARC Team follow-up sequence doesn't have to be an exact science. When you provide advance access, tell them the launch date. About a week ahead of launch, you can remind them one more time to encourage readers to wrap up their reading. That's not your cue to brow-beat them or guilt them into finishing your book. Keep the communication simple and to the point:

> Hey, [insert name], how are you coming along in reading my upcoming book? If you have any issues or questions, please reply to this email. Just a quick reminder the book will launch on [Insert book launch day]. Though I don't demand you leave a review on launch day, it'll sure go a long way in helping make this book a success.
>
> Thanks in advance,
>
> Dale L. Roberts

Swipe that copy or create something else in your voice. Giving your readers ample notice can help a little, but it's not mandatory. The next step is the most critical: launch day notifications.

On launch day, contact all your ARC readers and share the relevant links to your book. You can use a Universal Book Link (UBL) or a review-specific link to Amazon. The first option is free and quite simple to make.

Books2Read is a service provided by self-publishing distributors, Draft2Digital, that creates one link for accessing multiple retailers and region-specific redirection. When a reader uses this link, they'll arrive on a landing page with your book and all relevant retailer links. Once a reader clicks their preferred retailer, Books2Read redirects to their native marketplaces.

For instance, if you share a link to your book using the .com address, then readers will land in the US marketplace. Most of the time, Amazon prevents site visitors from outside a region from purchasing from another region. Rather than search for your book on their marketplace, they might pass or even think your book isn't available to them while not realizing they're in the wrong region to buy your book.

Universal book links are the best way to remove friction. Yes, the reader will have one extra click than if you were to give them a normal link, but most readers won't even notice or even care about it.

As of early 2025, Books2Read automatically searches for other retailers who fulfill ebook distribution beyond just Amazon. Print book and audiobook link options are available, but you have to enter links for those items to be displayed on your book's landing page.

Beyond that, Books2Read handles the links, directing readers to their region-specific retailer while tracking where they went. These insights show what platform performs the best for your book, so you can focus your marketing efforts through that avenue.

When your ARC reader uses your UBL, they go to the avenue they prefer to leave reviews. I encourage you to request readers to leave reviews where you want them most. Since this launch plan focuses on bestseller status for Amazon, you'll want to lean on your readers to post reviews there.

Encourage readers to leave reviews beyond Amazon if you're publishing wide (a gentle request can go a long way). Ask your readers and they might oblige. Don't ask? You'll never know if they'll go that extra mile.

The other way to direct your readers is by sending them a review-specific link to Amazon. Simply use the following link and add your book's ASIN (Amazon Standard Identification Number) at the end:

https://amazon.com/gp/product-review/

For example, to leave a review for *Wide Publishing for Books* on the US marketplace, you'd visit:

https://amazon.com/gp/product-review/B0CW1DZV6C

Amazon assigns an ASIN to your book when you launch or list it as a pre-order. You can find that ASIN in your KDP dashboard next to the book. ASINs vary per publication type, so you'll have a different ASIN for ebooks, print books, and audiobooks. You can't change this ASIN unless you delist the book, then re-upload it as a second edition.

The review link will work for every region. All you have to do is substitute ".com" with your region-specific marketplace (i.e., .co.uk, .it, .ca, etc.).

To create a universal review link, you can use the premium service Geniuslink. This link management tool allows users to create smart links that direct readers to the most relevant destination based on their location or device. It's like Books2Read, but it goes one step further by allowing you to create one link that'll redirect all readers to the region-specific marketplace and review section for your book on Amazon. Unfortunately, B2R doesn't have that feature, so if you want to remove as much friction as possible for the reader, you'll have to invest about $6 per month with Geniuslink.

To be clear, Geniuslink is not mandatory and may not be ideal for authors on a tight budget. Only invest in Geniuslink if you're confident you can cover the monthly fees long-term. While $72 per year isn't a significant amount, it could strain your author earnings if you're not careful.

In the event Geniuslink isn't in the cards for you, simply provide all region-specific review links to your readers and allow them to choose the one relevant to them. Or, you can always provide them with the universal book link and they'll figure out the rest. Again, I try to make it as simple as possible for the reader to post a review. Less friction potentially means more reviews.

VERIFIED PURCHASE REVIEWS VS. REGULAR REVIEWS

Amazon distinguishes customers who purchased a product through their marketplace and those who don't with a Verified Purchase stamp. This proof of purchase sits atop the posted review, acknowledging the customer bought the product on Amazon, therefore, what they say should be legit. That's not to say customers can't circumvent the reviews system through sketchy methods.

A few years ago, Amazon implemented a policy requiring customers to spend at least $50 in the past year in order to leave a review. This move aimed to block scammers and fake reviewers from manipulating the platform. When I first entered the business around 2014, anyone could leave a review, and some authors used unethical tactics to boost their book's ratings. These "black-hat" authors, who often look for loopholes or exploit the system for financial gain, would use click farms—services that create fake accounts—to artificially inflate their reviews. It worked for a while, which is why Amazon had to put a minimum spending requirement in place to ensure more authentic reviews.

I would argue that $50 is still a relatively low barrier to leave a review, so why not require customers to purchase the product before leaving one? Currently, customers can leave reviews without proof of purchase, as long as they meet the minimum $50 threshold. This policy might limit some ARC readers since they would need to have made a purchase that meets the $50 requirement in order to leave a review.

Enter the regular review or what some authors call an "unverified purchase" review. To be clear, an "unverified purchase" review comes with no stamp. The review simply posts with no formal stamp, hence why I just call it a regular review.

The more interesting factoid is how Amazon doesn't place any real value on one over the other. I'm not even sure customers pay attention to that Verified Purchase review stamp, since they're looking for answers or feedback that'll help them decide whether to buy.

It's not beyond Amazon to build a process around how reviews appear to customers. The more browsing customers select the "Helpful" button below a review, the more Amazon prioritizes that review. If you get a horrible review that gets a ton of votes for being helpful, then more customers will see that review. Conversely, if you get enough votes on positive reviews, it'll bolster those.

To be clear, customers still see all reviews, but they'll have to sift through the postings using a two-option filter or selecting the star rating. This is where things get really interesting.

Around 2019, Amazon implemented a new ratings system where customers can leave a rating without a review. I, among many other authors, felt a little upset at first, because now you have no context for how to improve your product. Reviews go a long way into not only selling more books but perfecting your backlog and upcoming publications.

With ratings, Amazon removed a lot of friction for the customer. In fact, Amazon encourages some customers to leave a star rating, followed by a gentle prompt to write a review. While they don't require customers to leave a review, the star rating itself contributes to the visibility and credibility of your product page.

Since nine out of ten customers look at reviews to make an informed purchase, Amazon wants your book to have some outside validation, even if there's no context. If you ever find yourself in need of more reviews, consider encouraging readers to leave a rating for your book. Not everyone wants the burden of justifying why they did or didn't like a book—they simply want to make their purchase and move on. Encourage ratings as an easier option for readers, and you may see more engagement.

GETTING VERIFIED PURCHASE REVIEWS

If you're looking to get more Verified Purchase reviews, you have a few options to run with:

1. Distributing gift copies
2. Limited-time discounts
3. Free promo upon launch (KDP Select only)

Distributing gift copies of your book can be a helpful strategy to get reviews, but it does come with some potential issues. When you buy gift copies on Amazon, you can either email a redemption code to the recipient or get the code to send out yourself. The cost of the gift copies will be the same as your ebook's price, but you'll receive royalties from that sale. While gifting copies is generally allowed by Amazon, it could create a direct relationship between you and the recipient, which may result in a biased review. Amazon has been known to reject or remove reviews they consider biased, though the exact criteria for this are not clearly disclosed.

Many authors have had success with this method, especially when distributing ARCs. However, the challenge lies in Amazon's unclear review vetting process. They don't always disclose how they determine whether a review is biased, so it's important to be cautious and ensure your process doesn't inadvertently violate any terms of service.

While authors can buy gift copies through Amazon, it's not the only option. You can also distribute copies directly to readers, bypassing

Amazon altogether. This method doesn't require any purchase, and you can send out copies yourself without spending money. When readers receive a gifted copy through Amazon, they may get the Verified Purchase stamp, adding some credibility to their review.

My preferred way to launch is through a limited-time discount on a pre-order or for the day after publishing. Having your ebook priced low bolsters sales and thereby spiking relevance in the Amazon algorithms. Then, Amazon shares your book with more customers, hoping to get additional revenue. Most people can't resist the bargain-basement pricing of an ebook.

Your ARC team doesn't have to purchase your ebook, but it certainly doesn't hurt to present the discounted offer if they'd like to further help the cause. I never require reviewers to purchase my book, whether free, discounted, or at a regular price. They chose to read and review my book, so I'm ecstatic whenever an ARC reader goes the extra mile to pick up a discounted copy.

As I always say, "Never expected, always appreciated."

When you notify your ARC team on launch day, mention the deal and explain how purchasing a copy can go a long way. It's going to be a delicate balance between gently suggesting and begging, so make sure you have an outside person to look over your request before sending it.

Similar to gifted copies, a discounted ebook purchase gives the review a Verified Purchase stamp. Again, the stamp isn't mandatory but could go some distance in building reader trust.

Another way to launch and get your ARC team to leave Verified Purchase reviews is through a free promo. This feature is only available through the KDP Select Program, which requires enrolling your ebook to access the five-day free promo option. The issue you'll have is timing since KDP will not allow you to post a free promo until your second full day after publication. To mitigate any issues, you could always notify your reviewers on day two of your launch.

Getting reviews on day one may not be absolutely critical to your success, but it certainly helps set you up for a stronger start. While securing purchases and gaining visibility in the New Releases category can give you a solid launch, having reviews early on plays a significant role in convincing more potential customers to buy your book. For a successful bestseller launch, reviews are an important part of the equation. As much as the sales drive the numbers, the credibility and social proof that reviews provide can make all the difference in shooting your book up the category bestseller lists.

Don't sweat it if you don't have a review plan for day two. While it's great to have reviews coming in right away, don't get discouraged if they don't. Focus on building your reviews over time, and you'll have more than enough for long-term success.

When you notify your ARC team, ask them to download a free copy during the promo dates so they can get the Verified Purchase review stamp. If they don't download the free promo copy, it's not the end of the world. Leaving a review is the most important part, and the Verified Purchase stamp is just a bonus.

I prefer doing the discounted ebook launch over the gifted copies or free promos. First, I'm already out more money through editing, formatting, and all the other expenses involved in self-publishing. Investing in gifted copies is an extra expense that has little return beyond the Verified Purchase stamp. Though some folks would argue having the stamp makes the review bulletproof, there isn't solid evidence to support that claim.

The KDP Select program is an option for authors to consider, especially if they have no intention of publishing their ebook beyond Amazon. Having your ebook enrolled in the program helps to launch at a greater advantage. Any time customers check out your book through Kindle Unlimited or Prime Reading, Amazon acknowledges that checkout as a sale in the Best Seller Ranking.

New authors should consider enrolling for the first ninety days of publication. Use the KDP Select Program to bolster rank through checkouts and sales on launch. Most authors should know if KDP Select is right for them within the first three months of publishing.

Since I have an established following, I don't use KDP Select for my books. Instead, I opt to publish my ebook on as many platforms as possible. While this wide approach to publishing may put me at a slight disadvantage compared to KDP Select-enrolled ebooks, I make up for it with steady sales. If my book can outperform KDP Select-enrolled ebooks, that's even better. Ultimately, my focus is on my book's performance: as long as I'm earning well and attracting new readers, that's all that matters.

Regardless of how you get reviews posted—Verified Purchase or regular—some will always be better than none. As a last resort, you can always fall back on requesting star ratings.

THE DANGERS OF ARC TEAMS

Distributing advanced reader copies makes a few authors leery about getting their work pirated before launch. If you're managing distribution of ARC copies through free services like Google Drive, you have some safeguards to consider. Though I'd love to tell you it's foolproof, the fact is, if someone wants to pirate your book, they will. As much as it is your job to write great books, pirates make it their mission to hack those same books.

I recommend if you're really concerned about having your work stolen, register a copyright for your book. Should you need to take legal action, you'll be ready with the registration in hand. You'll have an uphill battle without a legally registered copyright, so if you can afford the registration, get it.

The safeguards you can execute include a password lock you make only available to readers you've fully vetted or trust. Another way is to watermark your interior. Quite a few free online resources can help you sort that out. For me, I'd rather leave it up to the pros to manage my ebook distribution so I know precisely who has accessed my ebook, when, and if they have fulfilled their end of the bargain.

Services like StoryOrigin, BookFunnel, and Booksprout are premium author tools that distribute advance reader copies. Should you lack the funds to invest in their services, you can always consider distribution through free services like Payhip or Gumroad. These digital distribution services can watermark a PDF with the customer's email and name, making it nearly impossible to distribute without being caught. You'd just need to enable the watermark option when you're uploading.

PREMIUM SERVICES THAT GET YOU REVIEWERS

You'll find quite a few services that match your book up with volunteer readers who'll post a review. These services aren't ironclad, nor will they promise great results. What you get will vary from what another author will get. It's all about timing and interest. The better you package your book through a great cover design and compelling book description, the more likely they are to read it. These readers volunteer their time, so you can imagine they'll be a bit more discerning than the average reader.

Hidden Gems Books, NetGalley, BookSirens, and Booksprout are examples of premium services that get you reviewers. You will need to check with each platform well ahead of your launch. In fact, when I applied for an ARC team on Hidden Gems Books, it took over a year for me to get matched up. Even then, my results were modest at best, with Hidden Gems Books explaining that my nonfiction book wouldn't fare as well as fiction.

Places like NetGalley come at a higher premium, but you can look into a co-op service that divides the cost for shared access. When popular YouTuber Bethany Atazadeh recommended a NetGalley Co-Op hosted by Victory Editing, I was eager to try them out. In February 2025, the service was $57.75 per month or $500 per year, so I hopped onto it and found it quite useful. Normally, NetGalley charges $550 for six months of one listing, so you're saving over 50% by going with a co-op. (Please note, prices may change over time.)

You can use all the services you want from this list, but keep in mind that these will come at a greater cost. While book reviews can certainly help boost visibility, they shouldn't be the only thing you're investing in. Getting reviews is important, but it's just one piece of the puzzle. In the next section, we'll discuss other marketing strategies you can use alongside reviews to maximize your book's success.

I met an author who spent thousands on editorial reviews and premium review services. Her book tanked big time. She'd hedged all her bets on the success of her book, spending everything on reviews instead of distributing the funds across other marketing efforts. I felt bad for her because she invested all her money into one avenue, leaving nothing left for other strategies.

PREMIUM REVIEW SERVICES

Avoid premium review services that directly compensate readers when gathering reviews for your book. As mentioned previously, Amazon is wary of biased reviews, and paying readers to post reviews may lead to that bias. If you're considering paid review options, make sure the service you choose doesn't compensate the readers, but instead relies on volunteers. Editorial review platforms, like Kirkus Reviews, do compensate readers, but they provide professional reviews and aren't intended for mass, reader-driven review generation.

For example, you'll find some premium review services that'll get you a certain number of reviews on Amazon based on what you invest. These are a no-go and unacceptable by Amazon's review standards. Should you find a service promising you a certain number of reviews based on what you pay, ask them how they source readers and reviews. Ask them what happens if they don't get enough readers to fulfill your minimum review guarantee.

I spoke with one such premium review service provider and he openly admitted that he'd have one of his paid staff members handle any reviews to fulfill the guarantee. That's a no-go since that staff member is getting money for completing a review.

If you're ever concerned about a review service and unsure if it's a good fit, ask around the author community. Should you discover no one is using this service, then you might want to pass. Or double-check any service provider through the Alliance of Independent Authors' Watchdog List. Though the list isn't comprehensive, it has hundreds of premium services listed, along with a recommendation based on their research.

Editorial reviews are an exception to the rule of paid reviews. These reviews are from external sources, such as review services or recognized critics, and are great for adding third-party credibility to your book. Unlike customer reviews, which come directly from readers, editorial reviews are typically published on websites, social media, or retailer pages. Services like Kirkus Reviews, Readers' Favorite, provide premium review services that help build this credibility. You can share parts of these editorial reviews on your book's Amazon page (via Author Central) or on your website to boost your book's appeal. Editorial reviews play a role in building trust, but aren't necessarily the driving force behind achieving bestseller status—those depend more on customer reviews, sales, and visibility.

You will find several free and premium review sites and services when you visit DaleLinks.com/Reviews. I sorted the sites based on what they have available. For instance, one option is Book Award Pro, a service primarily focused on matchmaking for books to awards and reviews. Or you can test any of the review exchange platforms like Pubby.

With all the information you've learned so far, research the options at my link to make sure it's a good fit. For instance, I'm less likely to spend a ton of money on an editorial review that's posted on some random website visited by few people. If it's free, great! If it's $200, that's a hard pass.

Readers' Favorite provides one free book review for any books you submit, with no catch. While they may upsell other products and services, I've found their free review service sufficient for my needs. If you're in a pinch, you can opt for their expedited service, which guarantees quicker turnaround on reviews. These reviews are posted to sites like Goodreads, personal websites, and others, but not on Amazon. It's important to note that paying for this service isn't the same as paying for a review on Amazon, which would violate Amazon's Community Guidelines. Instead, the review appears on external platforms, providing third-party credibility and enhancing your book's visibility. You can also include these reviews in your book's Editorial Review section on Amazon, which helps boost discoverability and lends more trust to your book page.

ARE ARC TEAMS SAFE TO USE ON AMAZON?

I've heard a theory that Amazon is against ARC Teams and may even shadow ban books using this practice. This idea likely comes from authors speculating about how Amazon might react to ARC Teams, but in reality, I've known many authors who manage successful ARC Teams without any issues. The key question isn't whether authors have problems with managing ARC Teams, but whether it's safe to do so on Amazon.

Amazon never suggested that using ARC Teams violates their guidelines. In fact, some people confuse the rule about offering products in exchange for reviews. Amazon still permits the distribution of advance copies, as long as it complies with their Terms & Conditions. In their words:

> It's OK to review a free or discounted book (advanced reader copy) that you received from an author or publisher. However, they can't require a review in exchange or try to influence the review.[ix]

Amazon knows ARC teams are an effective marketing strategy and converts more browsing customers into buyers. The other products that are not books are problematic, so I imagine that's why they have this policy in place for giving away products to post reviews.

As long as your ARC Team consists entirely of avid, unbiased readers, your review gathering process should go flawlessly.

FRIENDS & FAMILY: WHY THEY WORK AGAINST YOUR MISSION

Though asking friends and family for support might seem like an easy option for new authors, I advise caution. Yes, having support from loved ones is valuable, but it can backfire if you aren't careful about who buys and reviews your book. Most of your friends and family likely aren't your ideal readers, which can negatively impact your reviews and undermine the third-party credibility of the feedback you receive.

Amazon's Customer Review policy states that they do not allow reviews from anyone perceived as having a close personal relationship with the author. This means anyone who shares a household should not leave a review. Also, if you've sent Amazon orders to an address, that may eliminate the review as well.

Should Amazon discover any direct relationship with the author and the reviewer, they'll reject or remove the review. While KDP doesn't appear to be terminating accounts because of biased book reviews, Amazon removes reviewing privileges should they detect a repeat offender. While this doesn't hurt you, it could certainly affect your close supporters.

I'd be remiss if I didn't disclose exactly what Amazon says about customer reviews.

> If we determine that you have attempted to manipulate reviews or violated our guidelines in any other manner, we may immediately suspend or terminate your Amazon privileges, remove reviews, and delist related products. In addition, if we determine that an Amazon account has been used to engage in review manipulation, remittances and payments may be withheld or forfeited.[x]

Rather than risk jeopardizing your credibility, avoid relying on friends and family for reviews. Focus on building a strong foundation of unbiased feedback from readers who truly connect with your book. This will allow your reputation to grow steadily over time.

I'll even suggest you should avoid having any friends and family support you through purchases on Amazon. Unless they're a diehard fan of your niche, they'll be doing a great disservice to your book's relevance in the Amazon algorithms.

For example, if my aunt loves to buy books about quilting, needlework, or crocheting, my book about fitness might not be a good fit for most readers of that type of content. Amazon's algorithms try to connect my aunt's love for all things sewing and my exercise books. If Amazon were to suggest my fitness books to other sewing fanatics, then chances are likely few people will buy.

Few readers cross over from one niche to the other. When Amazon makes a recommendation, they want it to convert to a sale. Should the recommendation fall on deaf ears, they're out money and you're out an opportunity.

If you really must have a loved one support you, consider having them work as part of your street team where they help promote your book to their friends, connections, or even at local libraries.

I stress the importance of not simply looking for the sale or review just anywhere. Consider the audience. Are they a good fit? Then, encourage them to buy. Are they loosely interested? Then, have them share it with folks through social media, email, or in-person. If they're *really* wanting to show support, then fulfill the order yourself. You can gift them a digital copy or offer to order a wholesale copy you'll autograph for them.

Many authors lose heart when their friends and family don't support them or buy their books. But this is actually okay, especially if you're aiming for Amazon to serve your book to the ideal buying audience, who might not be in your immediate circle.

REVIEWS WRAP-UP

You don't have to limit review gathering to the Amazon platform, though it helps immensely in driving sales in that marketplace. Think about hitting every major avenue like Goodreads, YouTube, websites, blogs, and even alternative retailers in Apple, Barnes & Noble, Kobo and more. Reviews are powerful marketing tools providing third-party credibility and social proof. Just a friendly reminder: Some reviews, regardless of where they're posted, are better than no reviews at all.

Consider using snippets or blurbs posted on other platforms in your Editorial Reviews section available through Amazon Author Central. The review must be relevant, and you have to credit the source.

Avoid putting snippets of reviews already available on Amazon. I tested out the theory that having more reviews readily available in the Editorial Reviews section but saw no major changes. Once I read the fine print, I realized this is a big no-no with Author Central. They don't want redundancies on your product page. Even though you might love that one review on Amazon that perfectly showcases what your book is all about, you simply shouldn't copy and paste that into your Editorial Reviews section.

Many authors make the mistake of writing the book and immediately hitting publish, but this is doing your work a great disservice. You need to get social proof so other readers are more inclined to buy and read your book. Getting reviews isn't that hard, but many authors choose to believe it's labor-intense or requires thousands of dollars. If you have some of the best practices and safeguards in place, you shouldn't have to work too hard to get your book the much needed love and attention it deserves.

Always plan your review gathering well ahead of launch, double check premium services for deadlines, and give ARC readers time to read and write a review before you hit that official launch button.

CHAPTER 4:
SET UP PRE-ORDERS

You need to create a lot of pre-launch buzz so when your book goes live on the Amazon Marketplace, it has better chances of success and discoverability. While you'll want to leverage every imaginable marketing tool and service you can for your launch, you'll first need a product page so you have a destination to send traffic.

Enter KDP pre-orders.

At the time of this writing, KDP only offers pre-orders for ebooks. When setting up a pre-order through KDP, you're simply getting a placeholder on their website. This product page is available to the public where customers can reserve a copy for download on launch day. All sales directly influence the Amazon Best Seller Rank (ABSR). While a fully launched book gets a thirty-day window in the New Release categories, pre-orders get the same. However, you get to double-dip since you have the New Release categories upon launch of the pre-order and again on the launch date.

You shouldn't go into this without a solid marketing plan though, because once your product page is live, Amazon's algorithms starting tracking sales. Should your pre-order sales tank, the algorithms are less likely to serve your book to potential customers. Keep reading; I've got more tips and insights to make the most of your book launch. As long as you're actively promoting your pre-order, you'll increase your chances of a successful launch and boost your book's visibility, putting you on track to hit bestseller status.

When the customer pre-orders your ebook, they do not get instant access. Instead, they put a hold on your title, so when the book is released, they get billed and then the product is delivered. On launch day, you'll see the sales start to pour in, with most of the pre-order sales being counted within the first 48 hours after the official release.

KDP EBOOK PRE-ORDER SET UP

In the first step of the upload process on KDP, at the bottom of the window you'll find the options:

- I am ready to release my book now
- Make my Kindle Ebook available for Pre-order

KDP allows you to schedule a pre-order for up to 365 days in advance and they'll even let you reschedule should you need to change the release date. They'll allow you to delay up to thirty days once without penalty.[xi] This one-time exception applies to your account, not just the postponed book, so only delay a pre-order if you absolutely have to.

You will lose your pre-order privileges should you cancel a release or delay it too many times. Amazon has to send out an email to any customers who bought your pre-order, which doesn't look too good on them. That's why their policy is understandable since they don't want to lose face because of somebody else's mistake.

CHAPTER 4: SET UP PRE-ORDERS

When I set up a pre-order, I only use my final draft. Quite a few authors will slip in a placeholder, but I've heard nightmarish stories of placeholder files, incomplete manuscripts, or unedited manuscripts being distributed. With all the hats indie authors wear, it's no surprise that some people will forget to upload the correct file. Conversely, Amazon is also prone to making mistakes. Rather than giving them anything less than my final draft, I give them exactly what the customer should receive so I won't make a mistake and they don't have a chance to either.

To fix any typos or minor errors in your manuscript, you have till the last three days before launch to upload the correct manuscript. Once that three-day window closes, whatever you last uploaded on KDP is what Amazon distributes. After it launches, you can correct it however many times you want. Just be aware your book will go through a vetting process before the updates push out to Amazon.

As for the rest of the upload and publishing process, it works like any normally published ebook on KDP. Fill out all the relevant metadata on the first step, upload your files on the second step, and set the pricing on the last step.

Remember, you'll have the choice to opt into KDP Select on the last step of publishing. Using KDP Select for your first ninety days puts your ebook at a greater advantage over other books. However, that benefit doesn't come until after the launch since readers don't officially get access to your book until launch day. Naturally, Amazon will not share your KDP Select-enrolled ebook until it's available in their subscription-based system.

For those of you who publish wide, do not opt into KDP Select if you want to distribute your ebook to other platforms (e.g.,

Draft2Digital, Apple, Kobo Writing Life, etc.). Enrolling in KDP Select gives Amazon exclusive digital rights for your book during the enrollment period, meaning your ebook cannot be published on other platforms, including your own website. Once the enrollment period ends, you can publish your ebook anywhere you'd like.

This agreement doesn't pertain to any print book or audiobook iterations of your publication. KDP Select covers just the single ebook title you've chosen to opt into the program, nothing else. If at any time you don't see value in the KDP Select program, simply opt out.

Visit your ebook title in the dashboard and hover over the ellipsis on the right, then choose "KDP Select Info." You'll go to the promotional page for that title and a pop-up will display your enrollment information. Clear the box next to **Automatically Renew**, and you're set. You will have to fulfill the rest of your enrollment before you can publish that ebook elsewhere. I always wait till the day after my enrollment period.

Amazon has web crawlers searching high and low for infractions, so do not play with them. Quite a few authors have faced serious consequences for running afoul of the KDP Select agreement, so tread carefully.

Should you want to remove your book from enrollment part way through an agreement, you'll have to contact KDP support. I'm guessing KDP isn't a big fan of closing out an agreement partway through, so only do it when you *absolutely* have to. When you pull out of enrollment prematurely, you may have to sacrifice all earnings for that agreement period.

If you plan to enroll in KDP Select, you still need to use the pre-order option for ebooks so you can start building buzz and driving

CHAPTER 4: SET UP PRE-ORDERS

traffic. I recommend having your ebook up for pre-order around thirty days before the launch date. This'll give you enough time to gather and execute your plans without freaking out if something slightly goes off the beaten path.

You are welcome to market and promote your ebook pre-order right away. In fact, you'll want to plan at least one promotional activity per day over that month to ensure consistent traffic flow to your product page.

The best way to entice more customers to pre-order your book is through a limited time discount. Unless you have a hardcore following in the thousands, price dropping is the best way to get more pre-orders. How much you discount the pre-order is entirely up to you, but keep in mind you'll have to change that price on launch day. After that, it'll take KDP about one to three days to update your pricing.

For example, I'll run a pre-order at $0.99. Since I can't change any of the information seventy-two hours before launch, I either have to update the pricing four days before launch or on launch day. KDP doesn't take too long to approve books with pricing updates. I've found it usually takes less than a day, but this could vary based on your timing and content.

Once the book is live, I'd kick it up to its full retail price of $7.99. This rough example isn't indicative of how you should price your ebook. If you want to launch at $9.99 and have a pre-order at $2.99, then go for it.

Communicate a sense of scarcity when promoting your pre-order, so people are more apt to act now rather than wait later when your pricing shoots up. You shouldn't put anything in your book description about pricing or a limited time deal; Amazon frowns upon this. Instead, you'll need to rely on outside resources to communicate this one-time price discount. Tap into your email list, social media, and any avenue you can to get the word out.

Pro tip: You'll find the best sales come on the last day if you've promoted your book enough in advance. Give everyone a few more reminders on the day before launch to drive additional sales. That momentum is going to propel you forward and get your book in front of more Amazon customers.

SCHEDULE PRINT BOOK LAUNCH

On the first step of the upload process for paperback and hardcover, you'll see one of the last options is for scheduling a release. Don't be confused; you aren't scheduling a pre-order; you're just setting the date for your print books to be available on the Amazon marketplace.

About one to two weeks before the launch of your ebook, schedule the print iterations in paperback and hardcover. For example, if you set your ebook to launch on June 1, you'd schedule your print books to launch on May 15. This two-week window gives your ARC readers the opportunity to post their reviews. This'll go a long way in providing social proof for anyone considering your ebook pre-order or for when the ebook launches.

Having reviews lined up before the official launch isn't mandatory but may get you a few extra sales leading up to and after your book launch date.

Scheduling your print books to launch one to two weeks before your ebook release—and after the pre-order phase—requires a bit more work. However, if you prefer to launch all iterations on the same day, you can schedule your print books for the last day of the pre-order phase. Fair warning: You won't have those reviews settling in until a day or two after launch, slowing down any momentum you could've otherwise had with advance launching your print books two weeks ahead.

For any authors wanting copies on-hand in time for an in-person event or a virtual launch party, give yourself at least one month lead time to account for printing and shipping times. Author copies do not come nearly as fast as Amazon's Prime 2-day shipping. It's been my experience that it takes roughly a week to two weeks for the print books to arrive at my house.

Side Note: You will not affect the Amazon Bestseller Rank for your book when buying author copies. You only influence your rank when buying books directly from the Amazon Marketplace. I wouldn't recommend using that to bolster rank. If you need one or two books within a couple of days, then order from Amazon. Otherwise, bulk order your print books from the last step of the upload process.

I totally understand that ordering author copies isn't in everyone's budgets, but I implore you to find a way to save up for it. While everything might look good on a computer screen, it can look *way* different in reality. And print quality will vary based on the region you order books. Color saturation and accuracy of cuts on the print books fluctuates, so do yourself a favor. Order at least one of every book you publish.

When you get your book in the mail, open it up and carefully inspect it. Read a few pages and flip through the entire book. Try to put yourself in your reader's shoes. Does everything look clean and readable? Do you notice any layout issues or even typos? Now is the time to get everything finely tuned and ready for the launch.

Technically, you can order proof copies from KDP before you even hit publish, but Amazon really ruins the product with a single-band watermark stretched across the top of the cover. Is it ideal? No.

I lean heavily in favor of scheduling a book because I have the option to order author copies. Compared to stopping short of publishing and order a watermarked copy, scheduling should be a bit more appealing to you by now.

To summarize: Schedule your print books to launch at least one to two weeks before the official ebook launch date to get your ARC readers to post reviews. To order author copies, set the scheduled date at least one month in advance to allow time for printing and shipping.

CHAPTER 5:
RUNNING AMAZON ADS

Amazon Advertising is available to anyone with an Amazon Kindle Direct Publishing account or an Author Central account. You can natively advertise your books on the Amazon platform to a warm audience. Compared to other ads platforms like Google and Facebook, Amazon Ads are much easier to navigate and, sometimes, more cost-effective.

Before diving into advertising your book, remember this one rule:

Do not invest any money you cannot afford to lose.

All paid advertising comes with its share of risks, especially if you don't know what you're doing. Although I'll give you a basic overview of running an Amazon ad, you might have a few questions beyond what I cover in this book. You can get all your questions answered and an understanding of the mechanics of Amazon ads in my two-time award-winning book, *Advertising for Books*.

One of the best resources in Amazon Advertising education is through their free certification courses. You can access them when you visit the question mark bubble in the top right corner of your ads dashboard. Amazon updates their courses regularly with new videos, written content, pop quizzes, and certification testing. I've picked up a few certifications over the years and find the platform continues to improve their educational resources.

WHEN SHOULD YOU RUN AMAZON ADS?

Many indie authors aren't sure when to start running paid ads. The answer is simple: once your product is listed on Amazon's website. Ideally, you should begin running ads during the pre-order phase of your ebook. This allows you to test and refine your targeting, optimizing your ads before your book officially launches. While it's important to have some best practices in place, you don't need to wait for everything to be perfect before you start advertising.

As mentioned previously, Amazon recommends making your book retail-ready to maximize the effectiveness of your ads, and this includes:

- 15 reviews or more with an average of 3.5 stars or greater
- A great description
- A high-quality cover image

After you launch your print books and before your ebook's launch day, you can have your ARC readers post their reviews. This will help build social proof, but don't wait for a specific number of reviews to accumulate—if you've put effort into creating an irresistible book, start running ads right away. The reviews will support your book, but they won't hinder your ad's ability to attract more readers.

You can still run ads if the print book is live, and the ebook is on pre-order. Running ads during the pre-order phase will give you valuable data that can help optimize your future ad campaigns once the ebook launches. For example, if your pre-order starts on June 1 for a July 1 ebook launch and your print books go live on June 15, you'll have two weeks to gather data from the pre-order ads. This allows you to create more effective ad campaigns for both the ebook and print versions once everything is officially available.

After the print books launch, you'd notify your ARC readers to post reviews. Having the reviews should give your ads a much better conversion rate since, as mentioned previously, nine out of ten people check reviews before purchasing a product on Amazon.

I recommend starting ads as soon as the print book is live or once you have around fifteen reviews, especially if you're working with a limited budget. Running ads without reviews is still a valid strategy, but having reviews can boost your odds of success by adding social proof. For new authors without a large following or an email list, ads can still drive traffic, but reviews will give you an edge in convincing potential buyers. If you have the budget to run ads, even without reviews, it can still be effective, though ideally, you want to balance your efforts with reviews posted.

WHAT TYPE OF ADS SHOULD YOU RUN?

The Sponsored Product ad is the best option for promoting your book on Amazon. They're simple to set up and manage. Any author with a deeper backlog of books can consider Sponsored Brand ads, but this promotes more than one of your books. However, I wouldn't recommend this ad type if you're looking to get targeted results for that new book.

Though I wish it were as simple as clicking a single button and my ad is running, it's actually a bit more complex. After clicking Create campaign and selecting Sponsored Products, you'll have nine additional steps to complete before your ad goes live.

Under Ad Format, you choose a standard ad or custom text ad. I choose the standard ad option since it doesn't require additional work to display your book to customers. The custom text option is where you provide ad copy of up to 150 characters. Personally, I've not seen a difference in conversion with or without ad copy. However, don't let that stop you from testing it out, especially if you've got a firm grasp on copywriting.

Next, you'll search for the book you wish to promote in the Products section. You must type your title exactly as it appears in your dashboard, including case-sensitivity. Or use your book's ASIN. Once you find and select it, move onto the Targeting section. I do not recommend advertising more than one book type within your ad group (a division of the ad campaign). You can create multiple ad groups in one campaign to separate the publication type. This helps you isolate any poor-performing targets and products without taking down the relevance of an ad.

For targeting, you have two options: automatic or manual. Anyone experienced in Amazon Ads can jump right to manual targeting since they are more precise and less expensive. For most everyone else, I recommend starting with automatic targeting where you give the ads platform control of what targets to share based on your book's keywords, categories, description, and other metadata.

Automatic targeting isn't perfect since Amazon's algorithms might tie your book to other less relevant targets. These targets include keywords or products. You're entirely responsible for sifting through what Amazon targets to find: poor converting targets, irrelevant targets, and high-performing targets (more on that later).

Because you're having Amazon source the targets for you, it makes setting up a manual targeting campaign that much easier. Once you find what does and doesn't convert to a sale, you can build a more effective ad that converts to more customers while mitigating ad spend.

In the next section, you'll set the default bid for your campaign; this is the minimum you're willing to pay for each customer who clicks your ad on Amazon. They'll suggest a bid, but you don't have to use it. You'll be able to determine if you set the bid at the right level after the campaign launches. For now, you can use the suggested bid as a general range.

Negative targeting takes up the next two sections for keywords and products. If you've run any previous campaigns and have poor-converting or irrelevant targets, here's where you place them. For instance, if Amazon serves my ad to customers searching "KDP login" for my book *Self-Publishing for New Authors*, I'd put that irrelevant target in the **Negative keyword targeting** section.

I can make that negative target an exact match or a phrase match. For exact matches, anytime a customer types a specific keyword with no deviation, Amazon won't serve that ad. With "KDP login", I'd put that as a **Negative exact**. This doesn't cover variations of that keyword, so if a customer types "Amazon KDP login to account", my ad will show up. That's why I can place "KDP login" as a phrase match, suppressing any variation of that keyword.

As your ads mature, you're going to find some ads won't convert with certain products. You'll insert that ASIN for that product in the **Negative product targeting** section. I've often put my own books into this section since customers already looking at my products are completely free. Why pay for that customer's click when they're already looking at my books?

If you set up the ad for custom text, the next section for Creative is where you put your ad copy of up to 150 characters. You'll even see an example of how your ad will appear on Amazon.

The Campaign section is where you can pick one of three bidding strategies:

1. Dynamic bids – up and down
2. Dynamic bids – down only
3. Fixed bids

The first option allows Amazon to raise your bid by a maximum of 100% if they believe it's likely to convert to a sale. Should they deem the ad less likely to convert, they'll lower the bid. Be careful in selecting this option because they can easily blow through your daily budget. Just because you're giving Amazon control doesn't mean they'll get the sale.

The other dynamic bids option is where they'll decrease a bid based on the ad being less likely to convert in a sale. I lean on this option quite a bit when setting up a campaign, but I have to trust they're not inadvertently suppressing my ad by bidding too low based on their algorithms determining the likelihood of a sale.

CHAPTER 5: RUNNING AMAZON ADS

Fixed bids give you full control. Whatever bid you set is what Amazon will stick to. There are exceptions to this rule if you've enabled other advanced options in your campaign (i.e., Budget rules, Bid adjustments). Should you want Amazon to push your ad out without adjusting your bid, this last option is for you.

After setting your bid strategy, you'll have the option to increase your bid on more favorable placement. This advanced option isn't one I recommend, since it requires more than a single chapter to explain. For now, leave that alone.

For the last section, you'll need to name your campaign, set a start and end date, and establish your daily budget. You can set it as low as $1 per day, but I recommend if you can afford it, increase it to $10 per day. At a buck a day, you will not see incredible results, but you will get some data from this campaign over the course of a month or two.

You'll expedite results with a bigger daily budget. When Amazon burns through your daily budget for the day, your ad will pause, slowing down any momentum it has. I recommend keeping your bid low and your daily budget higher. As you get more data after the ad launches, you'll be able to increase the bid to get your ad served to more customers.

Once you're set, click the Launch campaign button. Within a day, Amazon should have the ad posted on their site. You'll typically see results within the first few days, but it can take upwards of two weeks for your campaign to get any traction. You can gather all the information you need and create a high-converting ad by advertising well before your book launch.

The more books you sell through Amazon Ads, the more it increases your ABSR and the more likely your book will appear in front of relevant customers organically. When an ad converts more sales, Amazon places more relevance in your ad, therefore, allowing you to drop your bid. Ad placement is all based on a real-time, auction-based system, but the winning bid doesn't just go to the highest bidder; it goes to the ad most likely to convert into a sale.

Once your automatic targeting ad is out for two to four weeks, you should have enough data to launch a manual campaign. You'll use a combination of the Search Terms report and the Negative targeting from that ad to build out a manual campaign.

Visit the **Search terms** report regularly—at least once per week—to gather all targets used to serve your ad. You'll want to grab all the relevant, high-converting targets to seed the manual campaign. Then, gather a list of the low-converting or irrelevant targets to put into the Negative targeting section for the new manual campaign. This'll cut down your costs while increasing precision of who sees your ad.

Setting up a manual targeting campaign is almost the same as an automatic targeting campaign. After you select manual targeting, you can choose **Keyword targeting** or **Product targeting**. The targets you gathered from your automatic campaign will determine what you choose. You'll want about one to a dozen keyword targets. For products, you can select one to a dozen targets or a category. Do not go too overboard with categories; select one to two relevant options.

You'll still need to set the rest of the campaign like you did before with the bid, negative targeting, bidding strategy, and the settings. Once your campaign is live, you can always adjust it to better suit your needs from one week to the next.

A VIABLE ALTERNATIVE TO AUTOMATIC TARGETING CAMPAIGNS

Any time I've shared this strategy on my YouTube channel, I get occasional pushback from viewers stating that automatic targeting is a great way to lose money since Amazon is in control, not you. That's a fair argument for experienced advertisers, but what about anyone new to advertising? In order to fully understand how the platform functions, you need some form of "training wheels". That's where automatic targeting campaigns come in.

Let's assume you don't have the time to test ads and iterate. What do you do then? Grind it out and hope for the best? No, but you can try out a premium tool called Publisher Rocket. It's a tool that helps authors and publishers find profitable keywords, categories, and target audiences to optimize their book's visibility and sales on Amazon. One function within Publisher Rocket is for Amazon Ads.

You provide your book's ASIN and the software will provide potential targets to use for running manual targeting campaigns. Be selective with what you use because what you get isn't relevant to your book.

Also, less is more when selecting targets for your campaign. Even though you can have upwards of 1,000 targets, it's better to choose about one to a dozen targets, no more than 50 to 100. Providing too many targets within one campaign can confuse Amazon's algorithms since there's no clear direction for the ad. To make it easier on you, it's a smart idea to build separate ad groups or campaigns based on the type of target.

For example, in Publisher Rocket you'll get these types of targeting suggestions:

- Keywords

- Books
- Category Bestseller
- Comparable Author

The largest barrier of entry for Publisher Rocket is the retail cost: $199. I've had a license since 2017 and have more than made that money back while saving a ton of time in research. Whenever I want to skip automatic targeting, I dig out this tool and have it source the targets for me.

AUDITING YOUR ADS

Once your ad is up for a day or two, you can expect to see some results. The key indicators you need to pay closest attention to include:

- Impressions
- Clicks
- Sales
- ACoS (Advertising Cost of Sale)

Impressions are the number of times Amazon serves your ad in front of a customer. You don't pay a dime for impressions; it's essentially like free promotion. In the event you aren't seeing many impressions, your cost per click (your bid) is too low. Increase the bid a little at a time so that you aren't blowing through your daily budget.

Once you get plenty of impressions, you'll eventually get clicks. Unlike impressions, clicks will cost you every time. This is why you don't want to place your bid too high, because that comes from your bottom line. In the event you have a book that profits $3 per sale, you've got that much leeway to run a profitable ad. For example, a bid at $0.30 will get your roughly ten clicks in a day. Kick that up to a $1 bid, and you only have three clicks for the day.

The first example, you've got more opportunity to convert a sale. As long as you're converting at least one out of every ten clicks into a sale, you'll break even. For the higher bid, you have one in three chances. This is a huge reason I don't always lean in favor of the suggested bid: sometimes it's way beyond any level of profitability.

In the event you aren't getting clicks, then you've got one of three problems:

- Irrelevant target
- Poor converting target
- Unappealing cover design

Remember how I shared the importance of a high-quality cover design? This is where you can really tell if your cover is all it's cracked up to be. If your cover isn't enticing customers to click on your ad, then it's time to consider a redesign. But this'll only be after plenty of testing and research. Don't change your cover design every time your impressions aren't converting to sales. Once you have had time and experience with ads, you'll be able to know if it's a cover problem.

In the event you decide it's the target and not the cover, either remove the target if it's irrelevant or decrease the bid significantly if it's a poor converting target.

Once the clicks roll in, you'll want to focus on sales. If you're getting clicks, but few sales, you have one of a few problems:

- An unenticing book description
- Uncompetitive pricing

- Not enough reviews

Once a customer lands on your product page, they'll be using any of those options to make a purchasing decision. While the book cover got the customer to click the ad, if the book description can't give them a compelling reason to spend money and time on your book, then you just lost out on a sale.

Readers interested in your niche won't buy your book if you're not aligning your price point according to their expectations. This may apply when you're not pricing high enough or overpricing your book altogether. Try to closely match book pricing within your niche. Study the bestselling books in your niche and you'll get a clear sign of what readers are willing to spend.

Of course, we've already discussed the value of reviews, so try to get them loaded up right away and consistently.

When you see impressions that convert to clicks that convert to sales, you're on the right track. Visit your **Search terms** report at least once per week. Slip any poor converting or irrelevant targets into the **Negative targeting** section at the campaign level. This'll prevent any future ad groups from using that bad target within a campaign.

You'll also find some high-performing targets that'll help you build new manual campaigns or to add to current manual targeting campaigns.

WHAT NEXT?

Again, I highly recommend you avoid investing any more than you can stand to lose. You won't be likely to launch a campaign that's performing at its best on your first try. Give it time and plug into the free resources Amazon Advertising offers. I have a Discord community with over 1,100 active members; pop in to network and mastermind with other authors using Amazon Ads. It helps to share notes with your fellow authors and request feedback where needed. Trying to run ads on your own can be overwhelming and sometimes frustrating, so get with other authors to minimize stress and build your confidence.

CHAPTER 6:
PUBLISHING THE AUDIOBOOK

Publishing an audiobook may not always be easy or affordable, but it can help broaden your audience by catering to readers with different preferences—whether they enjoy ebooks, print books, or audiobooks. While an audiobook version doesn't affect your bestseller rank for ebooks or print books directly, audiobook sales can still increase your book's overall visibility and relevance in Amazon's algorithms. Audiobooks can attract more readers, and with the right marketing, they can lead to increased visibility and sales.

Let's say you publish your book, start running ads and sending traffic to your product page. When a potential customer lands on that page, what's the likelihood of them buying the book if there's only one product variation? Imagine the odds of someone buying the book if you have two versions (i.e., ebook, paperback). Now, let's add the hardcover and audiobook editions.

Giving your potential readers choices increases your odds of success. I, for one, am partial to ebooks and audiobooks. Having only the paperback or hardcover edition isn't enough to entice me. I simply don't want the material possession, so I'd pass on getting the book.

CHAPTER 5: PUBLISHING THE AUDIOBOOK

What if a customer loves only hardcover books and you offer just the ebook and paperback? Then, you've lost yet another opportunity to gain a new reader.

When you launch your book, consider making every available format accessible, even if it means delaying your publication date. By offering multiple formats—ebook, paperback, hardcover, and audiobook—you increase the chances of appealing to a wider range of readers. Having more product options gives customers the freedom to choose the format they prefer, which can boost your chances of making more sales and improving your overall visibility. When your ebook becomes a bestseller, Amazon is more likely to share it with a wider audience. Some of that audience may want something besides an ebook, such as a paperback, hardcover, or audiobook. This expanded reach gives you more opportunities to sell across all formats. When one iteration performs well, it can have a halo effect on the others, driving sales and increasing your visibility in the marketplace. This strategy can ultimately contribute to reaching bestseller status by appealing to a larger audience, which is the goal of a successful book launch.

In 2024, KDP offered closed beta access to a digital narration program where authors can have their ebook converted to an audiobook.[xii] Though artificial intelligence has been the talk of the town lately, it's far from perfect in many regards, especially what KDP offers. Yes, companies like ElevenLabs and Speechify have passable quality digital narration. The issue is you simply can't publish off-platform digital narration onto Amazon or Audible right now. It's either their tool or nothing at all. And even then, you have to get the invite.

The bottom line is: Don't ignore audiobooks. There's an eager audience just waiting for you to publish one.

THE TROUBLE WITH PUBLISHING AUDIOBOOKS

You can publish your ebook, paperback, and hardcover book through KDP and the product listing will appear on Amazon within one to three days. With audiobooks though? Not so much.

You first need to account for production time. For epic length novels, an author can expect it'll take weeks to complete, if not months, based on the production level (i.e., multi-voice actors, full cast productions).

Give yourself plenty of time before your publication date to complete your audiobook. Because once you have all the audio files, you still need to get approval from the self-publishing platform. Audiobook Creation Exchange (ACX) claims to process and approve audio files within ten business days, but I've seen it take weeks to months. Additionally, you cannot set an audiobook on pre-order or schedule it for a release date.

Timing your audiobook launch perfectly on your launch date is next to impossible, but there's one potential workaround: Findaway Voices by Spotify. This aggregate publishing platform publishes to nearly forty different online retailers, libraries, and subscription services. They reach nearly forty different platforms, including the only three avenues ACX reaches (Amazon, Audible, Apple).

Through Findaway Voices, you can set up pre-order. To my knowledge, the pre-order doesn't appear on Amazon or Audible, but it queues up those platforms for your book to go out around your launch date.

One major drawback of using Findaway Voices is you sacrifice some earnings in an 80/20 revenue split with them (in your favor). You could use both ACX and Findaway Voices, just deselect Amazon/

Audible through the latter option. But you run into the same issue of how slow ACX is in getting your audiobook on schedule.

PROMOTIONAL CODES: GREAT FOR GETTING REVIEWS

ACX provides authors up to 100 free promotional codes for the US and UK, as long as the audiobook is exclusive to their platform. These codes are great for distributing to ARC readers and encouraging them to leave reviews on Amazon.

If you choose to publish through Findaway Voices, you'll receive 100 promotional codes for Spotify, which can still be useful, but you'll need to direct your readers to leave reviews on Amazon, not Spotify. You can build an ARC team and provide these codes with the request for an Amazon review after they listen to your audiobook. Keep in mind that your ARC readers will need to meet the same review requirements as any other customer, ensuring that their feedback contributes to your success.

I often hear authors ask where else they can distribute their codes. Oh, man! Everywhere! More specifically, you can try:

- Facebook Groups relevant to your niche or dedicated to audiobooks
- Premium promo code distribution services (i.e., Audiobooks Unleashed, Book Blaze)
- StoryOrigin
- BookFunnel
- Your email list
- Social media
- Hosting a giveaway with other authors in your niche

- Give to librarians, local schools, and influencers

You won't have the opportunity to distribute promo codes until your book is live on the market, so this part of the review-gathering process happens after launch day. However, this step is crucial for maintaining your book's momentum. As reviews start rolling in, you'll create a steady stream of social proof that can help sustain sales and keep your book visible. Based on what I shared earlier about the conversion rate for ARC reviews, you should expect around thirty-three reviews to be posted on Amazon. Just like with ARC ebooks, promo codes are free, so once they're gone, they're gone. This continued feedback is an important part of maintaining the success of your launch and sustaining your bestseller status.

Communicate a sense of scarcity when sharing your offer for free access to your audiobook. Let them know what they stand to lose once all your codes run out. This is quite the opportunity; you just have to be open about it with your potential readers (well, it's technically listeners).

FINAL THOUGHTS ON AUDIOBOOKS

Audiobooks can be an important element of every author's book launch, but it's not always affordable or practical right away. If you can't afford to produce an audiobook initially, feel free to come back to it later. You can save a percentage of your ebook and print book earnings to reinvest into an audiobook down the line. While it's possible to launch a bestselling book without an audiobook edition, offering one could help attract more readers for years to come.

CHAPTER 7:
MARKETING & PROMOTION

Marketing and promotion are an inevitable part of every successful author business. Publishing and praying for bestseller status isn't a sound strategy. You will have to put in work beyond producing the book. In fact, any author wanting more sales needs to be as visible as possible. After all, that's what marketing and promotion is all about: visibility.

But where do you go and what should you do? Will it cost an exorbitant amount of money to market and promote your book? And what options will give you the greatest return on investment?

The overwhelming challenge of marketing and promoting books often causes authors to put in minimal or no effort. Just remember, something is better than nothing. If only you take away one point from this chapter, it's that if you're making a consistent effort, you're on the right path.

Make sure the efforts you're putting in are getting a worthwhile return on your investment, in time and money. This means you'll need to be calculated about what you do, focusing on cold, hard data to determine what is working and what isn't.

While I'll do my best to give you an array of options for marketing and promoting your book, I can't give you every imaginable avenue. Not to mention, marketing and promotion isn't one-size-fits-all. While I know quite a few authors who've had success with Amazon Advertising, quite a few others haven't. Sometimes it comes down to your understanding of what you're doing as well as timing.

THE LIST OF LISTS

The first task is going to take some time to work through, so you'll need to have everything ready well ahead of launching your pre-order. This section primarily focuses on using various free and premium book promotion sites, which are crucial for your book launch, whether or not you decide to discount your ebook or run a pre-order. Over the past decade, I've curated a list of over a half dozen reputable websites offering both free and paid book marketing services.

You can find this list at DaleLinks.com/BookPromos. While I would love to include it directly in the book, updating this list frequently would be impossible. These sites change their offerings and prices over time, so keeping the list current is best done online, where it's always up to date.

Create a separate document or spreadsheet to organize your research as you go, regardless of your specific promotional strategy. This will help you assess your options for future campaigns. Visit each site to determine if they're a good fit for your needs and note whether they're free or premium services. Pay close attention to the audience they serve—some sites specialize in specific genres and may not be useful for all types of books. For example, a site specializing in cowboy romance might not be helpful for a self-help book.

For instance, eReaderIQ offers free promotional services, but you'll have to contact them about how to list your book on their site. Whereas Bargain Booksy is a premium service that offers a range of prices depending on genre. Popular genres reach a bigger list of readers, therefore costs more.

When you've sifted through the list, you'll need to do a little more research to determine if it's a good fit. Word-of-mouth goes a long way, so ask around the author community to see what folks recommend or discourage you from using. Take every story with a grain of salt, because, as mentioned previously, marketing and promotion isn't one size fits all.

Next, you'll need to dig further into how a specific service reaches readers. Remember, just because these sites are on the list doesn't mean anyone is endorsing them. They're merely one of hundreds of options. Considering that anyone can set up a website and claim to be a book marketer, you'll need to be extra wary.

Ask these questions when vetting services for your book:

1. Does it cost anything?
2. How does the site reach readers?
3. Does your book fit on that platform?
4. What are the timing requirements?

I think we can all agree: If it's free, give it a shot. Just don't disregard the results after running a promotional campaign with a free service. Why spend any more time on a service that doesn't produce the results you're looking for? However, any free service is worth trying once.

The biggest area of concern is how a service reaches readers. Book promotion websites often rely on organic traffic, paid traffic, an email list, or social media to reach readers. Investigate what that reach is like. For instance, if their service includes promotions on a Facebook Business Profile, visit that page. The number of followers isn't as important as engagement. Thousands of followers don't mean a thing if no one is engaging in the posts. Without engagement, the platform's algorithms are less likely to push that post to a wider audience, therefore, it's wasted movement.

You'll also want to make sure you aren't promoting your book in the wrong avenues. Again, if you see a social media promotion service, study the books most featured on their feed. Pay closest attention to engagement again, because the posts that get the most engagement are powerful indicators of the audience this social media service reaches.

Last, identify timing requirements for each service provider. Some sites will take your deal the same day it's live and others require two weeks or more advance notice. This'll play a huge part in the next steps.

PLANNING & EXECUTING

Now that you have a custom list for your book, it's time to plan things out. Remember how I had you set up the pre-order two to four weeks before the launch date? Now I'm going to have you build out a daily action plan for promotion. This means you'll place one promotional service per day. I'd even recommend that you plan for a post-launch campaign lasting one to two weeks, so you keep the train rolling, even if you increase the price of your ebook.

Although Amazon thrives on sales, it relies on consistency even more. By lining up a promotional plan that pushes your book out daily, you're able to:

- Stay consistent with driving traffic and potential sales
- Monitor results

You could load up a ton of services in a single day—also known as stacking—but you won't know what is and isn't working. Once you've tried a service for the first time and seen the results, you can make an informed decision on what stays in future book promotions and what goes. Check your daily sales reports to determine how a campaign is performing and remember to account for any sales made through Amazon Ads (if you're using them), so you don't give credit to the wrong source.

In your custom list, track any sales made from the site so you know the best order to place the promotional services for future campaigns. For example, if I found Bargain Booksy brought me 125 sales and eReaderIQ brought 5 sales, I'd most likely stack those on a single day for a future promotional campaign. Or if I had 50 sales from Book Doggy, I'd put it on a separate day from Bargain Booksy since they both drive significant sales.

Of course, this is only theory you'd apply for future campaigns and not your upcoming one. For now, your schedule should look something like:

- Mon., June 1 – Bargain Booksy
- Tues., June 2 – BookDoggy
- Wed., June 3 – eReaderIQ
- Thu., June 4 – Crave Books
- Fri., June 5 – Books Go Social
- Sat., June 6 – Buck Books
- Sun., June 7 – TCK Publishing

This is only a rough example and not prescriptive. Use this framework to plan your promotional campaign leading up to and following the launch. The launch period includes not only the day of release but also the days and weeks after. To maintain consistent sales and stay at the top of your niche, it's important to keep promoting your book well beyond the initial launch. In fact, a successful launch involves ongoing efforts for at least a week or more after the release to build momentum and visibility.

OUTREACH

While the free and premium book promotion sites can be effective, don't limit yourself to simply using those services alone. You're going to need to do a little more research for where you can find your ideal reader, so you're even more visible. This is rather broad, so let's narrow down what outreach means and how you can best implement it within your action plan.

Outreach is simply connecting with people who are currently in front of your ideal reader. This includes social media influencers, niche-specific groups on Facebook or LinkedIn, authors in your niche, and relevant clubs or organizations for authors like you. Will you have to do some cold prospecting? Sure, but it's not as difficult as you'd think if you have a few best practices in place. And, if you're already active in any of those examples, it'll be dead simple to break the ice with a potential avenue of exposure.

For instance, even though *The Joe Rogan Experience* is a wildly popular podcast, I wouldn't consider it to be a good fit for my books about self-publishing. Sure, a segment of Rogan's audience might be interested in my books or expertise, but it's probably not the best use of my time or theirs since it's not the best fit. Podcasts like the *Sell More Books Show* or the *Indie Writers' Club* are a better fit, since their audiences are primarily authors.

It's better to appear on a podcast with a small, devoted following interested in your niche and not a massive podcast with a tenuous interest in your topic.

Before you look to schedule yourself on your favorite podcast or work with a social media influencer, you need to be prepared with a few essentials.

MUST-HAVES IN OUTREACH

Lead with your best foot anytime you're reaching out to potential collaborators. This means you should have a press kit ready—containing a few items that showcase you and your work—before you contact a single person.

A professional headshot goes a long way, but I realize hiring an experienced photographer can be out of budget for a lot of authors. In that case, use what resources you have available, like a smartphone camera. When you take a picture, stand in front of a neutral background so viewers focus on you, not distractions like a pile of laundry.

Craft a long and short bio so that potential interviewers have options for introducing you. Easily whip together a great bio with artificial intelligence, just make sure to thoroughly edit, revise, and seek feedback for it.

On the same document for the bio, include all relevant links to your site, book, and social media. For any author who feels extra ambitious, generate a nice one-page download of all that with Canva or Book Brush. That'll wow people on the first impression and only requires about ten minutes or so to create.

Create a folder on your computer with those items, this includes:

- Headshot
- A short and long bio
- Relevant links
- Book cover

Zip the folder and upload it to a cloud drive, then create a download link to share during your outreach.

One additional option to consider that'll make everyone's life easier: a scheduling app. There's nothing worse than playing schedule tag with someone. It wastes time and could lead to confusion with time zones and availability. A scheduling app removes most of the friction so instead of saying, "When are you available for an interview?" you can say, "Grab a time on my schedule."

I've used Calendly and SimplyBook.me, but you don't have to restrict yourself to those premium monthly services. AppSumo has an evergreen offer for their scheduling service called TidyCal. All three options allow you to sync with most calendar apps so you don't double book yourself. Heck, you can even close out days that you don't want to conduct an interview so that your host connects with you when the time is right.

Can you go without a scheduling app? Sure, but you'll find having a scheduler removes extra work so you can focus on other areas of marketing and promoting your book.

CHAPTER 7: MARKETING & PROMOTION

HOW DO YOU CONTACT SOMEONE?

It's dead simple to submit your book for a promotional service, whereas reaching out to someone you hardly know is a little intimidating. This shouldn't be an issue if you think about what you bring to the table. Of course, you want to push your latest book so you sell more copies, but most anyone can publish a book these days. You must answer one vital question on every person's mind when you're contacting them:

What's in it for me?

No, I don't mean you, the author, but me, the person who doesn't know you or know what I could gain by promoting your book. You must be able to succinctly describe why you're a valuable asset to the person you're contacting.

For instance, here's an email I'd send to a podcaster:

> Hey, Dale,
>
> I've been following your YouTube channel for some time now and love all the interviews you have with your guests. My favorite guest interviews were with Jonny Andrews, Jeanne De Vita, and Kris Austin. That last interview was one that convinced me to try Draft2Digital and I've loved the platform since.
>
> Knowing you're bombarded with guest interview requests regularly; I'll keep it simple. How do I apply to be on your show? I have an extensive background in writing and have also had three book awards for my work on publishing. I'd be happy to come chat more about my success in writing that your audience will find

> insightful and informative. And I'm even happy to share my interview across social media, on my website, and to my email list.
>
> Thoughts?

Admittedly, this isn't a masterclass in copywriting. Just keep your communication simple and brief. Frame your first contact like this:

1. How do you know the person?
2. What's one or two things you like about them?
3. What do you need to do to land an interview?

You will get a lot of rejections at first, but with consistent efforts, you'll build enough value online to entice people with a following to showcase who you are to their audience.

Once you get a response, only then can you hand off the press kit and book a time on their schedule. I usually defer to the organizer's schedule but also provide mine as an option. Remember, the less friction you have in the interaction, the better.

WHO DO YOU CONTACT?

Here's the primary concern I hear from most authors, and the answer isn't simple. You simply do a little sleuthing. Most interviewers, influencers, and connections are going to have a website with a contact form or, at the very least, an email address. You could direct message someone on social media, but I've found emails work best.

When in doubt, Google it out! It seems silly, but I've found just about anyone I needed to connect with through a Google search. Sure, I occasionally have to do some sifting, but it's minor work compared to the exposure and potential long-term relationships I can build with them.

WHAT IF THEY DON'T REPLY?

Don't be a nuisance. If they haven't responded after one follow-up email, then it's time to move on. You don't have the time to pester people for a potential interview. Your messages might've ended up in their spam folder, the timing might not be right, or they're just not interested.

One thing I can attest to as a host of a podcast, I'm more inclined to interview someone who is an active part of my community. Call it bias, but the fact is, when someone willingly contributes to my community, I'm happy to share them with my audience. That's because my viewers and community members already know this person and are happy to listen to this person talk on my podcast.

Think about a community you're part of online that is relevant to your niche. Is there someone in charge of a Facebook Group or Discord Community that serves as a mouthpiece for everyone? Do they have a podcast, YouTube channel, or email newsletter you can contribute to? If you don't know, find out.

A lot of outreach comes down to what you're willing to do to put yourself out there. You'll get a lot of rejections, but stick to it and you'll eventually see more breakthroughs. You'll find when you have one interview, you can share that to land another interview elsewhere since you have proof you're an invaluable guest.

Speaking of podcasts and outreach, I'd be remiss if I didn't share one of the best free resources for outreach: PodcastGuests.com.

PodcastGuests sends out an email twice per week with a list of guests looking for podcasts, and podcasts looking for guests. I've been following them for years and have landed dozens of interviews. Just a heads up though! You'll get an email every Monday and Thursday. Act right away! The email broadcast reaches over 30,000 subscribers, so podcasts get flooded with queries.

Hop into your email inbox and press the Ctrl and F keys. Instead of manually scrolling through emails, use the search feature to quickly find mentions of keywords like "author," "horror," or "science fiction"—whatever's relevant to your niche. This saves you time and avoids wasting seconds that can add up throughout the day.

I subscribed to PodcastGuests premium service, but didn't see any noticeable results. However, it's been quite a few years since then, so this option might be better.

AUTHOR COLLABORATIONS

For an easier approach to outreach, consider author collaborations like email newsletter swaps or group promos.

Newsletter swaps are when two authors share the other author's book in their respective email newsletters. It's a simple yet effective quid pro quo system. You do not have to have a massive list to get started, but you must have *a* list, nonetheless.

The harder part is finding authors who are relevant to your niche. Do not conduct newsletter swaps or group promos with authors that don't align with what you're writing. That clash might lead to poor results and a waste of everyone's time, whereas authors writing within the same genre will benefit from the cross pollination.

Line up as many newsletter swaps as you can before and after your book launch Much like the promotional services, spread your swaps out over time for even coverage. Check the results from each swap to determine what worked.

It's always a good idea to know how many email subscribers the author has and their average open rate. Having an email following doesn't automatically mean that they're doing a good job of engaging with their subscribers. It's better to have a 50% open rate with 1,000 email subscribers than to have a 0% open rate for 100,000. You'll notice this is similar to social media—bigger doesn't always mean better.

Avoid discounting authors who have a smaller email subscriber base. They might have a modest following now, but it might grow in due time. Your readers will appreciate the new author and you might make a new friend in that author.

Group promos are like newsletter swaps on steroids because you're working with a group of authors who collectively share a massive sale of books. T The key is to stick with other authors in your niche. Typically, group promos will feature books at a discount, but that's not always the case. I've taken part in group promos where it's a collection of books at the standard price and at a discounted price and have found both are effective in selling books.

This is also a great way to connect with more authors at one time. Once you work with them, you can always follow up with them later to arrange a newsletter swap aside from the group promo. It's kind of like speed dating for newsletter swaps.

Premium services like StoryOrigin and BookFunnel provide newsletter swap and group promo services where you access a marketplace of authors looking to do business. Sift through their lists regularly to scout opportunities. You'll want to arrange these newsletter swaps and group promos at least one month in advance of your launch, so everyone has time to prepare their campaigns. The only thing you'll need to do is agree to a date that's suitable to do your part in sharing their content.

Side note: You do NOT have to work with all authors. If the author isn't to your taste, don't do the swap.

Absolutely, fulfill your end of the bargain, so schedule the email newsletter swap ahead. If you're doing your email newsletters on a weekly basis, set a reminder to yourself in a calendar or on your smartphone.

ARE THERE MORE EFFICIENT WAYS OF OUTREACH?

There are certainly options worth pursuing out there, but few that I can speak on. Around 2020, I discovered a marketing tool called Storiad that had a deep contacts database and native email outreach. This company has since grown to support thousands of authors and host over 48,000 contacts from all walks, including social media influencers, bloggers, media professionals, and more. And they even narrow it down to unique niches and specific needs like book reviews.

I was fortunate to pick up a lifetime membership before they removed the option. Now, you'll have to pay about $29 per month for access. Keep in mind, I've greatly simplified what Storiad does, because they have other features that include AI assistance, marketing planner, profit/loss calculator, a customizable author website, and more.

Storiad has a free plan, but you will not get access to the contacts database or email integration. Those two items are worth the price of admission, especially if you use any of their email templates to seed out your email outreach. Yes, you should personalize each email sent to someone.

Worst-case scenario: You don't want to invest too much upfront in time and money, so what do you do? Hire a virtual assistant. There are quite a few inexpensive options for hiring a virtual assistant. Search for just about any online freelance marketplace and you'll find someone willing to do the work you don't want to at an affordable rate.

Make sure you cue up your virtual assistant with very detailed notes. I recommend recording yourself doing the process or explaining what you want. That way, any time you need to hire a virtual assistant to do outreach again later, you can share the video tutorial.

FINAL THOUGHTS ON MARKETING & PROMOTION

There is no secret to marketing and promotion. What works for one doesn't always work for all. The common denominator among bestselling authors, though, is their ability to consistently show up. Consistent visibility is the name of the game, so if you want more buyers and readers for your book upon launch, it's a good idea to get in front of your audience repeatedly.

The movie *Deadpool & Wolverine* became a smash hit upon its launch on July 22, 2024. For months prior to its launch, Ryan Reynolds and Hugh Jackman appeared everywhere to hype the release. Even after the movie launched, the two actors kept promoting the movie. Over the weekend the movie released, it earned an estimated $438 million globally. Then it went onto smash box office records earning over $1.3 billion.

Sure, we can credit the previous movies in the series and the star appeal, but we can't discount the fact that Reynolds and Jackman went out of their way to be highly visible and on everyone's radar.

Though most authors won't have the publicists or agents to manage the same press tour these actors went on, you have more than enough opportunity, regardless. You merely have to etch out the time and plan to contact the people you need to so you get your book in front of more potential readers.

Try to book your appearances and collaborations in the month leading up to and following your launch. Start with a manageable schedule, so if you can only do one interview per month, then that's fine. Or if all you can manage is a newsletter swap, then stick with that. Ease your way into things and be consistent with your marketing and promotion.

CHAPTER 8:
BOOK LAUNCH DAY

Now that you've handled all the hard work ahead of time, all you have to do are a few minor tasks to make your book launch day official. Of course, keep promoting your new book to the moon and back. This means keep your schedule on track for book promo services, newsletter swaps, group promos, and the like. It's easy to forget these items on launch day, so set yourself a reminder to avoid forgetting.

If you discounted your book price, now is a good time to increase it. Set up a free book promotion for any ebook enrolled in KDP Select. You should have about a twenty-four hours before you can do a free promotion. It's entirely up to you how long you want it available for free. If you're doing it so your ARC readers officially download a copy from Amazon to leave a Verified Purchase review, then one to two days should be sufficient.

I wouldn't recommend running a deep discount in the pre-order phase and then doing the free book promotion because this irritates readers who paid money for your book. Do one or the other, not both.

Your next step is to notify all ARC readers that your book is live. As a reminder, make sure to share your universal book link or the region-specific marketplace link for them to leave a review.

For platforms like StoryOrigin, you provide all relevant retail links, then it notifies your readers. StoryOrigin will notify any stragglers two weeks after launch. In the event a reader never posts a review, you'll know when they request access to your next book. It's entirely up to you if you approve or deny them.

Though I've mentioned ordering proof copies of your print books before launch, you *should* include ordering a copy of your ebook and audiobook. While you know how the story ends or the exact content in the book, it's important you do one final audit through the eyes of a customer. I've caught several errors just by ordering a copy after publishing my book. Yes, it costs money, but if you're running a discounted pre-order or a free book promotion in the first week, you can get it for next to nothing.

The same goes with audiobooks. Buy it. Listen to it one more time, even if you don't feel like it. You must experience what the listener does beyond the pre-publishing phase. It's better that you identify problems rather than a listener. And, keep in mind, if you're ordering a copy from Amazon or Audible, you'll get a portion of that in royalties.

WHAT ABOUT LAUNCH PARTIES?

Okay, despite what you might think of me based on my videos, I am not a party person. Maybe in my twenties to thirties, but these days? Not so much. All joking aside, many authors have big aspirations and massive expectations about how a book launch should be.

Should authors host a party at a local event center to kick off the book launch? Is there a local bookstore willing to host a signing? That's entirely up to you. I'm fortunate that I can easily throw book release parties on my YouTube channel and invite my community for fun things like trivia, a giveaway, or expert interviews. Any author that has a deep network of people—whether in person or online—should consider some event for their book launch. Just be prepared to juggle additional responsibilities on top of your already busy schedule.

The fact is, my first few #1 bestselling books came out with a whimper. Beyond my email subscribers and modest social media following getting a notification, I did nothing else beyond that. They were essentially low-key launches with little fanfare. This proves it's entirely possible to become a #1 bestselling author without having to get too extravagant.

However, it might be the difference-maker when you host a party of a hundred of your best friends, so don't discard the idea altogether. On that day, you have them either place an order in person or celebrate when the book goes live.

The bottom line is authors are entirely responsible for the success of their book launch. If you want to throw a party and know there's an eager audience, go for it!

TRACKING YOUR BESTSELLER STATUS

Once you pull the trigger on your pre-order, your book is already eligible for bestseller status on Amazon. Visit all region-specific sites for your book, then scroll down to the Product Details for the ABSR. If you're using KIP Scout, you'll see the current ABSR displayed near the book's title (desktop only). Be mindful of every iteration, but pay closest attention to the ebook, since it's possibly the lowest barrier of entry to publishing a #1 bestselling book.

Amazon updates its rankings every hour, so there's no need for you to refresh your page every minute for real-time ABSR. You can see a broader overview of ABSR for your books on Amazon, but it won't show you how it performs on a placement level in the category system. You'll just get the overall ABSR, which is good if you're really hitting the top of the charts.

Just a heads up though, Amazon has delayed changes in ranking before. Should you discover you're getting sales but the rank isn't changing, contact customer support for assistance. Give Amazon at least half a day to reflect changes in ABSR. After that, contact them should you not see any movement.

Also, if you search for your book on Amazon, your book might show up with the Best Seller tag on it. Grab a screenshot of your victory and share it with everyone. Remember, you chose up to three categories for each iteration of your book, so explore all three options to see how you placed.

Pro tip: When you visit the **Product Details** for your book, click on the category to visit the Amazon Best Seller List for that niche. Scroll partway down the page to see a display that says "New Releases." Click on that, and you'll see how your book is performing among the books released within the past thirty days. To be clear, your book must rank in the top 100 (or sometimes a smaller range) of the New Releases section for that category in order to be featured. Even if you don't hit #1 bestseller status right away, you still have bragging rights as one of the top books released in the past month. Snap a screenshot of that and use this as another way to market your book.

Do not drive yourself crazy by checking the bestseller rank every hour on the hour, which leads me to what you should not do after publishing your book.

WHAT NOT TO DO

Authors are free to do whatever they want once they launch their book, but I highly recommend avoiding a few things I've often seen done by new authors. Don't spam no-value posts on social media, because they're highly ineffective. Yes, your book is awesome, but you shouldn't say:

> *Hey, buy my new book for 99 cents on Amazon for a limited time. #spammy #indieauthors*

Sure, your cover might coax a few people, but the post is missing one vital element: engagement. Beyond your inner circle, this post is going to die a quick and painful death. And posts like this only get worse the more prolific you become.

> *Yes, Dale, we get it. You published your thirty-eighth book. We were good on twelve books, so it's a hard pass.*

They may not comment that on your post, but their silence will speak volumes. A dead post is time wasted, so don't even bother posting it if you don't have the intent to get engagement.

Consider instead on framing your book in a way that's enticing. Create intrigue through thought-provoking questions or polls that'll make people stop scrolling on social media and contribute to your more interesting conversation (that's not just about your book being on sale).

It could be a simple hook like:

POP QUIZ!

What's the biggest benefit of publishing wide?

1. More sales channels
2. Global library access
3. Diverse reader base
4. All the above

HINT: *Wide Publishing for Authors* covers this and so much more! Visit DaleLinks.com/WideBook to get my exact blueprint for wide publishing.

Or, if it's fiction:

POP QUIZ!

Which sci-fi fantasy author shaped the genre the most?

1. J.R.R. Tolkien
2. Isaac Asimov
3. Ursula K. Le Guin
4. Octavia E. Butler

HINT: *The Chronicles of Eldarion: Rise of the Shadow King* was inspired by legends like these! Who's your favorite? 🚀 Grab a copy at XYZ.com for 99 cents today only!

Any authors that are hamstrung on what to write for crafting engaging posts should consider AI. Feed all the details you need for AI to assist you with writing compelling copy. You will not get something perfect on the first try, so don't give up if the first few attempts come back with less than desirable results. Provide feedback and suggest changes to AI in order to make the content effective and to your liking.

When you do enough social media posts like this, track engagement and share the data with AI so it can adjust future posts to better suit your followers.

Also, a little touch goes a long way, so once you've posted your engaging content, find other relevant posts and people to engage with. That brief interaction is enough for someone to check out what you're doing and further aid in boosting your post. Don't spend hours doing this—only interact with posts you're genuinely interested in. Otherwise, skip it altogether.

You do *not* want to just find someone on social media minding their own business, beat them up to buy your book in their comments, then split. Yeah, that's a one-way trip to Blockedville. Avoid spamming your book everywhere; it's not a good look. Even if you hired a virtual assistant to shamelessly promote your book, it's still your book being slung around, so it all comes back to you.

Last, do NOT just publish and pray for the best. Now is the time for you to keep pushing through because if you want to launch your book as a #1 bestseller on Amazon, you must actively work on the *Bestseller Book Launch Plan*.

CHAPTER 9:
POST-BOOK LAUNCH ITEMS

It's officially the day after the book launch, so what comes next? It's pretty much more of the same. Maintain all promotional campaigns and actively seek opportunities to showcase you, as an author, so your book is more visible.

The areas you should shift your focus to include:

- Check your Amazon Bestseller Rank. Take screenshots for proof and share this exciting milestone with anyone who's willing to listen.
- Get more reviews. Never stop gathering reviews if you want your book to have a longer life cycle on Amazon. With hundreds of books publishing to their marketplace, the one differentiating factor from the rest is how many readers buy and review your book compared to those that publish their books and wait for passive reviews to show up.
- Scale your Amazon Ads. This takes time, money, and know-how, so tread carefully into deeper waters. Just because you spend $1,000 in a day doesn't mean you'll sell books. You

must incrementally work your way to a daily budget like that where the return on investment is equal to or greater than what you spend. Test, test, and test some more, then measure results at each stage so you can make more informed decisions with your ads.

- Book more interviews. These take time to build momentum but can play a large part in building a grassroots following. Keep at it, even though you might not see huge sales from it. Your efforts will compound if you don't give up.
- Keep building your email list. This is the lifeblood of any author's business, so do not take me lightly here. Create a call to action for subscribing to your email in your books, on social media, on your website, and even in your email signature. Collaborate with other authors in newsletter swaps to grow your subscriber base, further cementing your position as the go-to author in your niche.
- Remain flexible. You must be ready to bend when necessary. I've done dozens of book launches and each one has come with one hiccup or massive blunder. It happens! Learn from it, adjust for your next launch, and move on. No one takes your book launch as seriously as you do, so give yourself a little grace.

You can use a lot of the *Bestseller Book Launch Plan* at any time for your book, so adapt it as you see fit. The more books you publish, the sooner you'll discover what launch sequence works best for you based on your skill set, following, connections, and budget (including money and time). Be patient and diligent; hard work and consistency pay off. You just have to stick and stay; never give up.

CONCLUSION

Since publishing *Putting My Foot Down*, Brent Underwood went onto update his book to include context. His book expanded from being simply a device to expose Amazon's flawed ranking system into a full-fledged short read. Yeah, you can read it all in one sitting, and you just might laugh at some of the tomfoolery. Overall, he still gets his point across loud and clear but doesn't seem like a dick for doing it.

Some authors might feel Underwood diminished the value of bestseller status on Amazon, so what's the point of chasing after the title, anyway? Whereas another set of authors see value in any victory—whether big or small—in their self-publishing business.

If you're looking for a cheap win, you could try gaming the system like Brent did, but I'd stress caution before you do. Around mid-2023, Amazon KDP implemented a new categorization system that limited the author's choice to three different browse paths in their Primary Marketplace on Amazon. Beyond that, KDP assigns the most relevant categories in each region based on the native categories and keywords selected.

Two to three years prior to the new categorization system, scores of authors had their accounts suspended and even terminated—both wrongfully and justifiably—for selecting improper categories for their books. Quite a few stated they didn't even select their categories, while some selected all their categories, but didn't realize choosing the wrong one would lead to termination. If you don't want to end up like some of those authors, I highly recommend educating yourself as much as possible.

One of my preferred resources in self-publishing education is The Alliance of Independent Authors (ALLi). This nonprofit organization is run by authors, for authors. They'll provide insights and advice when Amazon wrongfully terminates account holders, helping them get back their accounts. I've always erred on the side of caution by getting an annual membership with ALLi at the Author level. Get details at my affiliate link: DaleLinks.com/ALLi. Just a heads up, that's an affiliate link, so I earn a commission on sales, but I fully support ALLi and everything they do for the indie author community.

With the new categorization system in place, the competition on Amazon seems stiffer than ever, so getting a quick victory like Underwood might be a bit of a long shot, especially if you don't want to draw the ire of KDP by improperly categorizing a book.

Is it still possible to become a bestselling author on Amazon? Absolutely! Your book's success hinges on preparation, and now that you've read this book, you have everything you need to move forward with your next launch. The only way to increase your confidence in the process is to actually do it.

Will your next book launch be perfect? Heck, no! Even traditional publishing companies don't get it right every time; and they have teams of experienced professionals to manage book launches. That's why you have to allow yourself permission to make a mistake or two on your next launch. As long as you slow down, take notes, and adjust course for your next publication, you'll be good to go. There's no real failure if you learn something in the process and grow from that understanding.

Should another author devalue the worth of bestseller status on Amazon, that's not your concern. You don't need to convince anyone else how great it is to be a bestselling author. If you see the value in it, then share it with the world. Those who understand will follow along. The rest? They're merely crabs in a bucket, looking to drag you back down to their level so you can be as miserable as them.

Ultimately, you need to ask yourself why launching a bestselling book is so important to you. What's it all for? Do you simply want the title just so you can forever proclaim to the world that you're a bestselling author? Or are you looking to reach more readers while earning a living from your work? The more meaning you attach to this goal, the easier it will be to stay motivated and proudly share your success

The biggest victory is in you showing up. Many writers aren't as brave as you have been in publishing your work into the world. Most people aspire to write a book, and some couldn't even fathom seeing it published. You exceeded all those expectations and are going to shatter even more soon with the *Bestseller Book Launch Plan*.

Till then, happy publishing and here's to wishing you the best in your next book launch!

THE BESTSELLER BOOK LAUNCH CHECKLIST

I completely understand you just drank from a massive firehose of information, so you might want to have your work laid out for you in concise bullet points. That's why I whipped together this checklist based on everything shared in this book. You can get a simplified and abbreviated version of the Bestseller Book Launch Checklist when you subscribe to my email newsletter at DaleLinks.com/Checklist.

For a more granular view of the launch sequence, follow the steps in this checklist:

1. Lay the Groundwork
    - ☐ Research relevant keywords with KIP Scout or Publisher Rocket
    - ☐ Create a solid cover design
    - ☐ Write a compelling book description

2. Build an ARC Team
    - ☐ Recruit and organize your ARC team

- [ ] Distribute advance copies
- [ ] Communicate and follow-up for reviews

3. Set Up Pre-Orders

   - [ ] Set up a pre-order for your discounted ebook at least one month ahead of launch
   - [ ] Schedule your print books to launch two weeks before the ebook to collect reviews
   - [ ] Publish the audiobook

4. Run Amazon Ads

   - [ ] Create an Automatic Targeting Campaign for a Sponsored Product ad
   - [ ] Harvest high-performing targets and low-performing or irrelevant targets
   - [ ] After two to four weeks, build a Manual Targeting Campaign based on the data gathered from the first campaign

5. Marketing & Promotion

   - [ ] Sift the List of Book Promo Lists at DaleLinks.com/BookPromos and develop a plan to use free and premium services to promote your book every day before and at least two weeks after launch.
   - [ ] Build an email list and collaborate with niche-relevant authors
   - [ ] Create and execute a daily, weekly or monthly action plan for outreach

6. Book Launch Day

    - ☐ Increase the ebook pricing OR run a Free Book Promotion with KDP Select
    - ☐ Notify your ARC team to post reviews
    - ☐ Track your Amazon Best Seller Rank (ABSR) and grab a screenshot of your success

7. Post-Book Launch Day

    - ☐ Continue monitoring promotional campaigns and ABSR
    - ☐ Gather more reviews
    - ☐ Keep building your email list

8. Analyze & Adjust Future Campaigns

    - ☐ Check daily sales reports and Amazon Ads
    - ☐ Determine what worked best and troubleshoot what didn't work
    - ☐ Adjust your game plan for future book launches

A SMALL ASK

Your opinion matters! Whether you loved the book, found it helpful, or have suggestions, leaving a review wherever you purchased or downloaded it makes a huge difference. Reviews help other readers discover great books and give me valuable feedback to continue improving my work. I read every review and truly appreciate your time and input. Post a review at DaleLinks.com/BestsellerReview or your preferred website.

If you're hungry for more self-publishing insights, check out my other books at DaleLinks.com/Bookshelf. Also, feel free to connect with me directly or ask questions by joining my Discord community at DaleLinks.com/Discord.

Thank you for being part of my author journey!

ABOUT THE AUTHOR

Dale L. Roberts is a self-publishing advocate, award-winning author, and trusted voice in the indie publishing community. With over 50 titles, 40 literary awards, and a YouTube audience of over 100,000 subscribers, Dale is a go-to authority for self-publishing success. His most recent book, *Self-Publishing for New Authors*, is an entrant for the 2025 Pulitzer Prize for General Nonfiction.

As a Video Content Advisor for the Alliance of Independent Authors and a pioneer in video marketing for authors, Dale empowers writers to build their brands and achieve bestseller status. His journey from a struggling first-time author to a self-publishing success story inspires thousands worldwide.

Relevant links:

- Website – SelfPublishingWithDale.com
- YouTube – YouTube.com/SelfPublishingWithDale
- My Books – DaleLinks.com/Bookshelf
- Discord – Dalelinks.com/Discord

ABOUT THE AUTHOR

- Facebook – Facebook.com/SelfPubWithDale
- X (Twitter) – X.com/SelfPubWithDale
- Instagram – Instagram.com/SelfPubWithDale

SPECIAL THANKS

After interviewing over 125 different authors on my two YouTube channels, reading dozens of books about self-publishing, taking a handful of courses on the subject, and consuming from a host of online resources, I can't even begin to thank every person without leaving someone out.

I'll keep it simple and thank the person who was directly responsible for my success in self-publishing and indirectly responsible for me getting into YouTube video content creation—Jason Bracht. Though he hasn't been active in the business in quite a few years, his influence left an indelible impression and lasting impact on my life as a small business owner and person. His generosity and compassion for others knows no bounds, so I'm forever grateful to Jason for what he gave to me so early in my career.

And my wife, I have to add my wife. What, do you think I'm crazy?! She'll never read this thank you page, but just in case she does—thank you, Kelli.

Big thank you to my beta readers, William D. Latoria, Ava Fails, and Ansley Dauenhauer. Without your keen eye for detail, this book wouldn't be what it is now.

SPECIAL THANKS

And, of course, my writing mentor and editor, Jeanne De Vita. I can't say enough kind words about this woman! If you want to be a better, more confident writer, see Jeanne.

RESOURCES

I'm so glad you took the time to flip to the back of the book to check for links and referenced resources. If you're looking for the citations, you'll need to move to the last chapter of this book. Otherwise, you'll find a list of books, tools, resources, videos, sites, and services. Rather than clutter up the book with a ton of links, I figured this would be the cleanest way to share what I was talking about all in one place, in alphabetical order. Please note that some of the links are part of affiliate programs, and I may receive compensation for any sales made through them. This doesn't affect the cost to you but greatly helps contribute to the research and publishing of books like this one.

These resources are here to help you take the next step, whether it's diving deeper into the topics covered or finding the tools that best suit your needs. Enjoy!

REFERENCED BOOKS

- *Amazon Keywords for Books* by Dale L. Roberts – Dalelinks.com/KeywordsBook
- *Advertising for Books* by Dale L. Roberts – DaleLinks.com/AdsBook

RESOURCES

- *How to Write a Sizzling Synopsis* by Bryan Cohen – DaleLinks.com/Sizzling
- *Putting My Foot Down* by Brent Underwood – DaleLinks.com/FootDown
- *Mastering Amazon Descriptions* by Brian Meeks – DaleLinks.com/MeeksBook
- *Sales Copy Unleashed* by Robert Ryan – Sales Copy Unleashed
- *Wide Publishing for Books* by Dale L. Roberts – DaleLinks.com/WideBook

REFERENCED AUTHOR TOOLS & RESOURCES

- ALLi's Watchdog List – DaleLinks.com/Watchdog
- Amazon Advertising Certification Courses – LearningConsole.AmazonAdvertising.com
- Amazon: Send to Kindle – Amazon.com/SendToKindle
- Books2Read – Books2Read.com
- DIY Book Covers with Derek Murphy – DIYBookCovers.com
- Kindlepreneur: Amazon Book Sales Calculator – DaleLinks.com/Calculator
- My List of Lists for Book Promos – DaleLinks.com/BookPromos
- My List of Review Sites & Services – DaleLinks.com/Reviews
- Publisher Rocket – DaleLinks.com/Rocket

REFERENCED SITES & SERVICES

- The Alliance of Independent Authors – DaleLinks.com/ALLi
- Audiobooks Unleashed – AudiobooksUnleashed.com/Add-An-Audiobook/
- Book Award Pro – DaleLinks.com/BookAwardPro
- Book Brush – BookBrush.com
- BookBlaze – BookBlaze.co
- BookFunnel – BookFunnel.com
- BookSirens – BookSirens.com
- BookSprout – DaleLinks.com/BookSprout
- Canva – DaleLinks.com/Canva
- Draft2Digital – DaleLinks.com/D2D
- eBookFairs – DaleLinks.com/eBookFairs
- ElevenLabs – ElevenLabs.io
- Geniuslink – DaleLinks.com/Genius
- Gumroad – DaleLinks.com/Gumroad
- Hidden Gems Books – HiddenGemsBooks.com
- Joe Solari – JoeSolari.com
- KDP – KDP.Amazon.com
- Kindlepreneur – Kindlepreneur.com
- KIP Scout – DaleLinks.com/Scout
- MailerLite – DaleLinks.com/MailerLite
- My Vetted List of Cover Designers
    - Dibbly (fka The Urban Writers) – DaleLinks.com/UrbanWriters
    - GetCovers – DaleLinks.com/GetCovers

RESOURCES

- o Miblart – DaleLinks.com/Miblart (my go-to cover designer service)
- Payhip – DaleLinks.com/Payhip
- PodcastGuests – PodcastGuests.com
- Pubby – Pubby.co
- Readers' Favorite Free Book Review – ReadersFavorite.com/Book-Reviews.htm
- SimplyBook.me – DaleLinks.com/Simply
- Speechify – Speechify.com
- Storiad – DaleLinks.com/Storiad
- StoryOrigin – DaleLinks.com/StoryOrigin
- TidyCal – DaleLinks.com/TidyCal
- Victory Editing – DaleLinks.com/NetGalleyCoOp

REFERENCED VIDEOS

- Bethany Atazadeh: *I Tried NetGalley as an Indie Author so YOU Don't Have to… But seriously…* – DaleLinks.com/Bethany
- Dale L. Roberts: *I Paid 5 Designers to Create the Same Cover* – DaleLinks.com/5Designs

REFERENCES

i   Underwood, B. (31 Jan 2017). Behind the Scam: What Does It Take to Be a 'Best-Selling Author'? $3 and 5 Minutes. https://medium.com/the-mission/behind-the-scam-what-does-it-take-to-be-a-best-selling-author-3-and-5-minutes-ec05cee1749a

ii   Amazon.com, Inc. (27 September 2024). Kindle Direct Publishing Terms and Conditions. https://kdp.amazon.com/terms-and-conditions

iii   Amazon.com, Inc. (no date). Amazon Store & Detail Page > Sales Ranking. https://kdp.amazon.com/en_US/help/topic/G201648140

iv   Justia. (29 December 1986). Blatty v. New York Times Co. (1986). https://law.justia.com/cases/california/supreme-court/3d/42/1033.html

v   Amazon.com, Inc. (no date). Amazon Store & Detail Page > KDP Categories. https://kdp.amazon.com/en_US/help/topic/G200652170

vi   Noblit, C. (17 December 2024). KDP Global Fund Payouts [Updated December 2024]. https://www.writtenwordmedia.com/kdp-global-fund-payouts/.

REFERENCES

vii   Solari, J. (no date). A Smaller Slice of a Shrinking Kindle Select Pie. https://joesolari.com/a-smaller-slice-of-a-shrinking-kindle-select-pie/

viii   Chesson, D. (21 January 2025). Kindle Keywords: Insights From 100+ Published Authors. https://kindlepreneur.com/7-kindle-keywords/

ix   Amazon.com, Inc. (no date). Site Features > Amazon Community > Community Guidelines. https://www.amazon.com/gp/help/customer/display.html?nodeId=GLHXEX85MENUE4XF

x   Amazon.com, Inc. (no date). Site Features > Amazon Community > Anti-Manipulation Policy for Customer Reviews. https://www.amazon.com/gp/help/customer/display.html?ref_=hp_left_v4_sib&nodeId=G8CXDFT9GLRRSV3G

xi   Amazon.com, Inc. (no date). KDP Publishing > Create a Book > Book Detail Resources > Kindle eBook Pre-Order. https://kdp.amazon.com/en_US/help/topic/G201499380

xii   Amazon.com, Inc. (1 November 2023). Invite-Only KDP Beta for Audiobooks. https://www.kdpcommunity.com/s/article/Invite-Only-KDP-Beta-for-Audiobooks?language=en_US

www.ingramcontent.com/pod-product-compliance
Lightning Source LLC
Chambersburg PA
CBHW071715020426
42333CB00017B/2276